Above the Battle

Above the Battle
The Personal Recollections of an R.F.C.
Scout Pilot During the First World War

Vivian Drake

Above the Battle
The Personal Recollections of an R.F.C. Scout Pilot During the First World War
by Vivian Drake

First published under the title
Above the Battle

Leonaur is an imprint of Oakpast Ltd

Copyright in this form © 2013 Oakpast Ltd

ISBN: 978-1-78282-160-1 (hardcover)
ISBN: 978-1-78282-161-8 (softcover)

http://www.leonaur.com

Publisher's Notes

The views expressed in this book are not necessarily those of the publisher.

Contents

Introduction	7
First Experiences	9
Training	20
Overseas	39
France	47
Over the Lines	51
A Bomb Raid	57
Scrapping	65
Mainly About Two-Seaters	70
A Night Stunt	77
Artillery Control	83
The Day's Work	94
Zep Strafing	119
The Somme	128
The Red Cross Machine	143

Introduction

The word Romance, and all it means, is so closely allied to the average conception of the present day war pilot that the layman can scarcely visualise the many sides of military aviation alone, nor yet the immense growth of the corps to which he belongs.

From an inconsiderable beginning—inconsiderable in the light of our present size—with few machines and few aerodromes, has grown a mighty organisation; and from a mere handful of pioneers there has arisen a vast band whose deeds have created a great Flying Service. In France, Russia, Italy, Egypt, Mesopotamia, Macedonia and Syria the pilots of the Royal Flying Corps have fought the enemy and wrung from him the uttermost respect for the familiar red, white and blue rings. But this respect and our supremacy has not been won without many a bitter struggle; and it is the details of the ever changing phases of aerial warfare which, even if described with a truth akin to baldness, are by far stranger than fiction.

At the outset of the war, seventy or eighty miles an hour was thought quite fast; a height of fifteen thousand feet was a vision to conjure with. Yet now, machines are often doing their every day jobs at twenty and twenty-two thousand feet, and flying at an air speed of 140 to 160 miles an hour—speeds not only commonplace but inevitably to be supplanted by speeds even more staggering.

Again, it is amazing, even when in his company at the Front, to step back out of the world of flying, so to speak, and survey the modern Flying Officer. A few short months before, and he had probably never even sat in an aeroplane or known how and why it flew. Yet now he regards a fight conducted at nearly three miles a minute, and three and a half miles above the earth as the veriest commonplace, scarcely worthy of mention, while all the technical business connected with artillery control, reconnaissance, photography, gunnery, bombing, etc., is to him an open book! But to a Flying Officer the nature of his training has rendered the metamorphosis as absorbing and seemingly natural as it is surprising to the onlooker.

Predominant amongst types, war flying has always drawn the man of action; above all else, it has appealed to the lover of individual adventure and initiative. And today, even though our flying operations are on a scale almost undreamt of before the war, the watchlike precision of the huge flying organisation has in no way lessened a pilot's unbounded scope, but rather increased it. As in no other arm is a man's initiative and grasp of an unusual situation called upon. The very nature and setting of his work affords opportunities for individual distinction which flying of necessity renders unparalleled.

But it must not be supposed that a pilot is allowed to fly about over the Front haphazard. Far from it. His very flight is part of one huge programme. On his shoulders there rests a real and potential responsibility which is very great indeed. Amidst a great battle situations may arise which test his capacity to the full, and upon his handling of the case may depend the lives of thousands of men and the fate of an entire sector.

Therefore it may be interesting to take a peep at bow he is trained, how he copes with events on the Front, and how he lives and works—and plays. However, it must be borne in mind that air work is of such a magnitude that it is impossible to review it individually and yet collectively, and that this book necessarily deals in small quantities.

Just latterly, the army and navy sides of aviation, in the shape of the Royal Flying Corps and the Royal Naval Air Service, have been merged together into a Third Service—the Royal Air Force. Speaking of the new organisation, it suffices to say that the very intimacy and company of the men, who have made the traditions attaching to their old services, engenders that which guarantees the future of the new one—a passionate *esprit-de-corps*.

C. G. Hoare.

May, 1918.

CHAPTER 1

First Experiences

.... Transfer having been approved, he should report to the School of Military Aeronautics on the date mentioned.

Such was the ending to the War Office letter relating to my transfer from my regiment to the Royal Flying Corps. Having passed an extremely searching medical examination, together with a few other preliminaries, an afternoon in the spring found me descending from the train at a small university town in southern England, where the aforesaid School of Military Aeronautics had its being.

With the help of Time, Providence, and a Ford (the second much necessitated by the third) I arrived outside a building which bore the magical inscription, "Adjutant, Royal Flying Corps."

I believe a number of wags had suggested to the adjutant that he might improve the shining hour by placing a truthful if not cheering inscription above the door, similar to the one carved on the dungeons of the Tower of London, "*Give up hope all Ye that enter here.*" This suggestion, however, had apparently not been approved by the adjutant, who continued to lurk inside his official web without warning, to young aerial *debutantes!* I eagerly pushed through these grim portals, expecting to be greeted by some urbane and pleasant officer. This idea was speedily scouted by a small corporal, who, looking me over as a butcher might a sheep before he slaughtered it, pushed a large book to me, saying, "Sign here, sir, please."

From my signature he then made out a small card, giving my name. Regiment, and "Course" at the school, at the same time presenting me with several closely typed sheets of foolscap which advertised themselves to be "Standing Orders." This beneficent youth closed his services to me by telling me where to go to get my quarters.

Again employing the three powers which I mentioned before, I presently pulled up outside what was evidently a university college. Here I was taken charge of by another, but older and fatter, corporal, who having ushered me up to a small unfurnished room overlooking the quadrangle, left me standing in the middle of it with my trunks, feeling somewhat lonely.

My arrival at the school reminded me tremendously of old school days, or more particularly one's first entry into a public school, when one is absolutely unknown and feels an extraordinarily minute particle of humanity! After a long period with my regiment, where we had been a small but very happy family, and where every officer knew his brother officers and men well, I experienced, I suppose, a homesick feeling. I think it was at this moment I felt my first and last regret at joining the corps.

After unpacking my goods and chattels, I sat down to read the voluminous Standing Orders with which I had been presented. I felt somewhat crestfallen at the end of this task, chiefly because there seemed to be little left to the discretion of officers. Numberless "do's and don't's" relating to everything from cheques to discipline, were set forth, and in fact I came to the conclusion that if the officers strictly obeyed all those orders that the Royal Flying Corps must be peopled by extremely pious and elderly aviators! (Experience has taught me what extraordinary conclusions a man can make.) These orders, however, were very wise when one remembers the type of officer which the Royal Flying Corps was fortunate enough to secure.

Flying naturally draws to it the youthful side of the army and a side which is often (thank heaven) tinged with reckless impetuosity. Herding together three or four hundred officers of this type, free from regimental trammels, and then working them extremely hard, was not unlikely to cause many an exuberance of healthy animal spirits, off, or for the matter of that, on duty. Any lack of complete discipline, even though a breakage of same was only thoughtless, would have greatly endangered the efficiency of the school, which had a severe task set in front of it in teaching these youths the large number of highly technical subjects which are so necessary for a modern war pilot to be conversant with.

The system of instruction was clearly set forth in programmes of work posted up in the lobbies of the college. I was staggered by the list of subjects with which I was confronted; they ranged from rigging down through fitting, meteorology, photography, military law, bomb dropping, wireless, artillery, cooperation, theory of flight, Morse code to astronomy, etc! Previous to this I had had no idea that a pilot needed to know much except actual piloting, and yet all this was apparently going to be crammed into a few short weeks! I anticipated "some" work!

The dinner bell cut short my reflections at this point and I moved over toward the mess.

The hall was used as a dining room and all the officers used to wait in a crowd at the foot of the staircase leading to it, for the commandant, or if he was not present, the adjutant, to precede them in to dinner. At this time of the day, when work was over and the long summer evening to come high spirits were the order. I have seen one or two humorous things happen at the bottom of this staircase, the chief one of which was when the commandant, who was very strict about discipline, after making his way through the crowd to the foot of the stairs was immediately shot up about six of them in a bound by a terrific surge of officers, who did it of course, by mistake! The unfortunate people in the front rank received the vials of his wrath, while the real culprits who had done the pushing at the back of the crowd nearly burst with suppressed laughter.

The mess consists of three very long tables running the ent.re length of the hall, and at the top of the centre table sat the commandant with the staff. The commandant very rightly insisted upon mess etiquette being observed in a proper manner, but this was sometimes a little difficult owing to the very large number of men sitting down to meals at once. In this respect officers were prone to develop a habit of coming in late for dinner so that the waiters, having served all the main body looked after them pretty swiftly. The authorities countered this by making a mess rule that an officer coming in late for dinner must start at whatever course was then being served. This was made the subject of a screamingly funny drawing by an officer artist, who portrayed a disconsolate looking officer being gravely served by a mess waiter with a "*demi-tasse*" as the only nourishment that could then be provided! This drawing was hung in the mess and caused a great deal of amusement.

The next morning we started our first day of the instructional course. Our day was spaced something after the following. From 6:30 to 7:15 a.m. we drilled, after that came breakfast, followed at 8:30 by a general parade. After this parade, lectures of various kinds took place until 12 o'clock, when we dismissed for lunch, to recommence at 2 o'clock for more lectures or practical work as the case might be, dismissing for toe day at 5 o'clock. During the evening it was generally necessary to write up and commit to memory the notes taken during the day's lectures.

Accordingly I "fell in" on parade with several hundred other officers at 6:30 a. m. A very smart non-commissioned officer was in charge of the drill parade and it was his task to test all the officers as to their ability to give and take drill orders absolutely accurately. Considering that every officer had been commissioned for quite a length of time, this drill seemed at first to be unnecessary, but first attempts showed this to be a very erroneous impression. Infantry drill only is used in the Flying Corps, but large numbers of officers had come from units other than infantry; therefore, their first few efforts of drill did not seem what one would have expected. The sight of infantry, cavalry, yeoman, engineers, and gunner officers, with perhaps a sprinkling of the Army Service Corps, Grave Diggers Battalion, and Canal Transport representatives, all trying to be smart and intelligent, was a fearful and wonderful sight!

All went well until the sergeant major essayed a somewhat ambitious movement with us, with the result that the adjutant, who was watching the proceedings, stood completely hypnotised by the strange spectacle which unfolded itself before his horror-stricken eyes, while the sergeant major, who was of the "Get a move on, damn your eyes" type, was nearly bereft of his reason in his efforts to restrain his language to the kind generally reserved for officers. Worse, however, was yet to come, for the sergeant major had been provided with a roll of officers, and he proceeded to call them out one after the other, working alphabetically, to drill the rest.

I can imagine a no more awful ordeal than the one gone through by the first man, a timid young cavalry officer of a bashful and retiring disposition, who, on his name being bawled out by the sergeant major, slunk dejectedly out in front of the parade his state of mind not being improved by the cold and glittering eye of the somewhat warlike adjutant.

The sergeant major, in tones which he probably meant to be *sotto voce*, but what in reality were quite distinct a quarter of a mile away, said, "Move them to the right in column, sir."

The cavalry officer, with frenzied courage "Move them the right to fours."

"As you were!" shrieked the sergeant major, while numberless trees were observed to shake with the concussion. "Move *to* the right *in* fours, sir."

With this assistance our unfortunate taskmaster got us moving and pointed approximately in the right direction. The poor wretch was then confronted by a far worse problem, that of having several hundred troops moving towards certain destruction at the hands of a barbed wire fence and not being quite certain how to turn them away or stop them! With the aid of more stage whispers from the sergeant major he eventually got us back, bruised but not beaten, to our original position, and, having received a tremendously military salute from the sergeant major which nearly frightened him out of his wits, retired precipitously to the rear rank, there to enjoy the next man's torture.

Being a mounted officer myself, and as my name stood painfully early on the alphabetical list, I made frantic endeavours to learn all I could. I had, of course, been taught infantry drill as well as my own, but as equally, "of course," forgotten it. I may also say it is quite one thing to drill men and make them do it properly and quite another to suddenly be called upon to go and do it yourself! I accordingly rehearsed to myself my "lines," and then awaited with what calmness I could the dread summons of the call boy (the sergeant major).

A few mornings later it came and I marched out in front of the parade having distinctly in my mind exactly what to say, turned round and faced them, and immediately forgot all I had taken such pains to learn!

"Move them to the left in line." This movement I accomplished with great skill, but my hopes were rather dashed by being asked to make them "About turn."

This brought before my rapidly glazing eyes one of the most awful dilemmas that confronts a nervous man on the drill field, that of getting the men facing you with the front rank in front! It is a bitter moment when after finally bringing your column to rest you see the hateful face of a man you know to be on the rear rank gazing blatantly at you from the front rank! Especially as the men always seem to wear an injured and pained look of having to submit to your mediocre efforts.

However, I had one of those streaks of luck which come so rarely in a man's lifetime, and to the astonishment of all concerned, when the final word "Halt" was given, the front rank was actually in front of the rear rank, and the right flank was actually upon the right.

Feeling that I had the histrionic range of Sir Henry Irving at least,

I walked proudly back to my place, having been officially passed—in "Squad drill duties." This was a wonderful thing as it meant that one could lie snugly in bed, while less cunning brother officers snuffed the morning air at 6:30 promptly!

After this drill the next great event of the day was the 8:30 instructional parade. All officers had to be present, exceedingly "properly dressed," for the inspection of the eagle eyed and ubiquitous adjutant. I mention this officer a good many times. Chiefly, I suppose, because he made a great impression upon me, as being a very fine specimen of the best type of British Regular officer. He always looked a soldier and a gentleman. His dress reduced some of our military dandies to tears of mortification, and his general manner induced the utmost respect, which was well deserved.

His life at the school cannot have been a very happy one, for at all times, on and off duty, he had to be the absolute model in however trivial matter for all the others to copy. He carried out this duty in a way which caused him to be liked and admired by every officer with whom he came in contact.

However, to return to the parade. Commandant's Daily Orders having been read, we were dismissed and told to proceed to the class rooms to which the programmes of work assigned us. My first morning's instruction was given by a sergeant mechanic to about a dozen of us. Sitting down with the actual engine in front of us he proceeded methodically to go through it from one end of it to the other, while we took down notes, asked questions and generally absorbed the whole thing. This instructor, in common with all the others I had studied under, had most skilfully reduced his subject to a very understandable and interesting lecture, during which, providing one paid attention, one could not help learning all about the subject in hand. The notes we took were of course invaluable for refreshing our memory, because we flitted so rapidly from one subject to the other that to trust to one's memory alone would have been, I think, fatal.

After lunch we proceeded to our first lesson on the construction of an aeroplane, the lecturer and his class having the actual aeroplane in front of them so that all points gone over were dealt with in a practical fashion. At the end of the day we were started off on the Morse Code. Little electrical instruments consisting of the Morse key, connected to a contrivance which emitted a buzz when the key was pressed, were issued to us, and with these we used to slowly spell out words to each other during the evening. Another officer and I rigged up, with the aid of some cheap wire, an electrical connection between our rooms so that we could buzz to each other without being able to speak, thus ensuring all communications being done by Morse Code only. This worked out very well and we both passed our tests very easily. We left the contrivance fitted up ready for people who came after us, and I have been amused on many occasions afterwards by officers saying, when we were introduced to each other, "Oh, aren't you the man who fitted up the buzzing contrivance at the School of Military Aeronautics?"

Lectures were also given to us *en masse* on various subjects, the most interesting naturally being those connected with actual flying at the Front. We all had the greatest reverence for officers who possessed the much coveted "wings" (the cloth badge of a full-blown pilot, worn on the left breast of his tunic) and we used to listen spellbound to any pilot who had been overseas, if we could get him to talk about the Front and his experiences there.

I think we all regarded overseas pilots as supermen!

We thus "carried on" day by day, working steadily through the programme allotted us, until the time for our examinations began to draw near, and our work naturally became more intensive on account of this. Our heads were now crammed with information on a good many subjects. We usually worked in pairs and compared notes late into the night, either in our rooms, or in a canoe or boat on the river. On Sundays we were allowed to relax and pursue our own inclinations, a wise concession on the part of the commandant, who realised that a man can produce a much better result if given a little rest between the cramming.

This relaxation in the case of a great number of officers took the form of a spin on their motorcycles. There were a great many of these fearsome instruments owned by pupils, who used to park them outside the college. It was unfortunate for the adjutant that the window of his room overlooked the chosen spot, as directly an instructional period was over the various owners would come tearing back from the lecture rooms, and finish up with a last thunderous spasm of noise from their exhaust, just under his window! In addition to this, it naturally became the practice for the officers to sally out, smoking, after dinner, and languidly examine each other's mounts, talking learnedly about valve clearances, piston rings, speed tyres, brands of oil and such technicalities. The discussion generally led to the remark "how much can she do?" Always answered by some wildly hyperbolic figure.

The querist was then prone to request to be allowed to "try her for a moment" upon which there followed (if the owner was fool enough to allow it) a perfectly fiendish uproar while the tester tore up and down with his cut-out wide open.

All this eventually became too much of a nuisance for even the very tolerant adjutant and his fiat came forth accordingly, to the effect that these dreadful monsters might only be kept providing they were garaged in an official garage, which the adjutant selected in an obscure part of the town.

Therein the enthusiasts used to gather of an evening, to listen uninterruptedly in an ecstasy of joy to the revolting clamour of each other's machines and technical jargon, with beatified faces.

However, with whatever contempt or sarcasm one may pour on this type of enthusiast, he generally made a very good flying officer, as the ownership of successive brands of motorcycle and car, with all their attendant troubles, which it was his joy to personally conquer, helped him tremendously with aero engines, while the nerve required to drive them at the speed he generally favoured argued well for a steady head in the air.

As I have said, our instruction proceeded smoothly on, day by day, but none the less eventfully. Fresh subjects, fresh lecturers, an occasional unexpected test of our knowledge, kept us constantly on the *qui vive*. The non-commissioned officer instructors as a whole contrived to make themselves wonderfully interesting, an accomplishment which the reader will better appreciate if he endeavours to imagine himself lecturing about the same engine in the same way to absolute novices, and to patiently answer all their silly questions, day after day, week after week, and month after month!

Regarding the lectures given by officers, pilots' lectures, on whatever subject, were naturally more interesting, as all the pupils always hoped that he would digress from technical subjects and talk about flying at the Front. This they sometimes did, and were then carefully egged on by a series of skilful inquiries until long past the time they should have finished.

Out of the volume of general information in this respect many, many invaluable hints could be collected—hints which were probably forgotten for several months, but which echoed back at some touch and go moment and enabled one to do the right, or nearly the right, thing.

There was one lecture which met with the whole hearted, if silent, approval of all the pupils. This was "Military Law" and the adjutant was "billed" to appear. To start with, the manual of Military Law was to us a most humorous, useful, uninteresting and altogether Satanically contrived volume! In a moment of weakness one might unguardedly open it and start to read. Chance might lead one to a dissertation on the size of officers' trousers buttons, or on the other hand one might thrill with the account of evidence of one John Doe, a full Private of the Line, whose trial took place in seventeen umpty-umph, for murder; the idea being that if the reader was at any time confronted by some similar humorist, that he might tell the latter exactly what to expect! I believe the volume is most interesting to numbers of old and grizzled colonels, probably graded as deputy assistant acting *pro forma ipso facto* adjutant generals, who, squatting in their dens on the —nth floor of the War Office, decided the fate of some unhappy soldier accused of stealing an egg, etc.!

However, to proceed. The adjutant entered the room. Silence! The adjutant mounted the platform, and sat down at the table. More silence! He opened his volume of *Military Law*. More, but this time uneasy, Silence!

If the adjutant had been asked as to what he considered the most horrible job he could have been doomed to, he would probably have selected the one which now confronted him.

He began. "Now, gentlemen, you can well realise that it is most necessary that you should understand Military Law. We will therefore deal with some supposed cases. Now, supposing one of your men were to give back chat to a non-commissioned officer; all we have to do is to look up the offence in the index, turn to the page, and we shall there see our course of action clearly dictated. Now then, turn to—" He started to look up the index himself.

Forty-five minutes later, he was doing exactly the same thing, not having opened his mouth! The pupils in the meantime discussing in whispers whatever subject was nearest their heart, or else trying to suppress their mirth over certain parts of Military Law not usually discussed in polite society!

At the end of this altogether successful lecture, the adjutant closed the book, and looking as if his mind had considerably bent itself against the grim rock which he held in his hand, said:

"The lecture is completed, gentlemen," and stalked out of the door with the dignity which only he could assume under such conditions.

The morning had dawned upon which we were to be examined.

One could almost hear the loud buzz of hundreds of brains striving to remember in what orbit Jupiter moved, and what was the valve clearance of a Renault motor, with all the other subjects tucked in between. Nine o'clock found us sitting in a large and rather beautiful organ hall, deprived of our best friends—our note books, and about to be issued with the first two papers both of which related to engines. The chief examiner sat on a raised platform overlooking us, while his fellow conspirators handed round neatly typed lists of questions.

Until I read this list I had never imagined what a number of uncertainties there were connected with the subject, or how wonderfully it lent itself to queries. I did not feel particularly mirthful, but was consoled by failing to discover any particular sign of joy anywhere else! I ploughed on for the ensuing three hours, describing quite minutely things I was sure I didn't know; and perhaps omitting things I did. I had to grudgingly admit that, to the man who simply remembered all that had been taught him, the paper presented no difficulties, and that it was altogether a rather sensible lot of questions.

At 12 o'clock, having completed "Engines," I tried to cast all thought of them from my mind and to concentrate on the next subject. At 2 o'clock we recommenced on Wireless, Photography, and other Black Arts. We waded through these and crept away to dinner feeling considerably enervated, and with the prospect of another day of it to come.

Dinner that night was very curious, as every man was asking every other man "how he got on" sometimes stating his full opinion of a question and the man who had propounded it. We naturally all felt that we had failed. After dinner the school resolved itself into two elements of thought, the first of which considered that an evening of hard study was the only thing that would pull them through the next day, while the other element was equally decided that it would go mad if it did the same, and that a brisk evening at the theatre or movies would be a much better course of action! Which I did I leave to your imagination.

To cut a long story short, we eventually finished all our examinations. The results were speedily published and to the gratification of everyone there were very few failures. The examination generally had been of necessity fairly searching, but no attempts had been made to "catch out" pupils. The school staff, with its experience of war, knew exactly how much it was necessary for a pilot to know, and while sternly insisting upon him knowing it, they realised that many a man may know a subject but yet be unable to explain it coherently to anyone else. Now came the terrific business of being posted away to an aerodrome to fly. We were allowed to state our wishes as to localities, and if it was convenient and efficient a man was sent to the aerodrome of his desire.

I was very keen indeed to get the very best flying experience I could before I went to France, and I accordingly applied to be posted to a certain great flying aerodrome, where I knew I was absolutely certain of this. Some of the social lights were fearfully keen upon aerodromes near London, for obvious reasons! Others wanted to go to aerodromes which happened to be near their homes, etc.

Most of us were given leave immediately after the examination pending vacancies at flying fields. I, therefore, departed for Scotland and arrived there the next morning. It was absolutely wonderful to be back amongst the dear grey hills and burns and glens which I love better than anything else on earth (although I am not a Scotchman) after the terrific hum and scuffle of the School of Military Aeronautics.

After a good bath and a better breakfast, I sallied out with a fly rod, with the intent to do to death various mountain trout, but above all to the company of —— well, never mind! Another story!

After an Elysian hour, perhaps not altogether connected with trout, I was rudely crashed back to earth by a small and rubicund youth, who inquired in a squeaky voice "'oo I was." I told him. His reply was to hand me an official telegram.

Report back absolutely immediately for posting to Flying Duty.
Officer Commanding School of Military Aeronautics.

Thus was my Elysia blasted! With a last long farewell—to the hills, of course—I started on a car to catch the south-bound express, and reported back the next morning proceeded straight to the adjutant's office, where he gave me printed orders to report to the commandant of the aerodrome I had desired to go to.

He shook hands with me, and with a kindly word or two in my ears I left his office, sincerely hoping that I should meet him again at some time or other. That afternoon a fast train bore me rapidly towards a place wherein I had put a hundred anticipations, hopes, and resolutions; a place wherein I was to do all that is romantic, exciting, and altogether absorbing—fly!

Chapter 2

Training

After having reported to the commandant's office, where I was presented with a card stating my name, a Pilot's Log Book, and injunctions to report to a certain squadron commander at 5 p. m., I proceeded to stroll round the great air station.

The landing ground consisted of about half-mile square of flat grass land, running down one side of which were a line of large hangars (aeroplane sheds) built on to a pavement which allowed the machines to be moved about easily in and out of the sheds. Each hangar had room for about six machines and various little offices, etc. Behind the hangars lay the main body of the camp, consisting of red-roofed stone buildings—barracks, messes, officers' quarters, repair sections, and all sorts of places—intersected by beautiful cement roads.

Tennis courts were laid out in front of the non-commissioned officers' quarters for their use and the men's. Some way further back, in a little hollow, more courts were provided for officers. It all looked quite peaceful on the hot summer afternoon, as no flying was taking place.

Continuing my perambulations I presently came to the officers' quarters and found my room. It was situated in a longish wooden hut raised several feet from the ground. A corridor ran straight down one side and electric light was laid on into each of the dozen small rooms it contained. I found my room furnished with a stove, army bedstead, table and chair and washstand. It looked pretty bare in spite of the fact that the usual quartermaster's notice was hung on the wall stating that the room was furnished with apparently quite a long list of objects. An examination of the list proved itself to be fairly accurate, although the objects were so inconsiderable as not to be noticed, such as:

Shovels, coal, officers, 1.

Blind, roller, spring, 1.
Poker, fire, officers, 1,

And so on and so on, until at the bottom it even listed itself as:
List, furniture, rooms of, officers, 1.

Quite cheered up by the perusal of this comic document, I set about unpacking my kit, of which, having been in the army sometime, I had naturally accumulated quite an amount.

My faithful folding canvas bath having performed its useful duty I hied me forth to the mess which was quite close by, with a very sound idea of having some tea. This accomplished it was nearly 5 o'clock, so I sallied out to the tarmac, moderately clean on the outside and with a huge tea on the inside, ready to attempt to fly, crash or do whatever else was in fashion.

The squadron commander proved to be a rather worried looking flying officer. He gave me the impression of having flown so much that he was positively uneasy on the ground!

He wore an inconceivably black and oily Flying Corps tunic with hat to match, which bore mute evidence of the hours he had sat behind oily engines. After a few leading questions he said: "All right, you had better go and sit down outside with the other fellows and watch the flying—if you use your eyes and your brains you be able to pick up quite a lot about how to fly, and occasionally how not to. I'll take you up later on in the evening when it's calmer."

I found about a dozen young officers sitting down outside the hangar, looking on while the mechanics started up engines, the machines having just been brought out.

They were quite a jolly looking lot and typical of the officers the Royal Flying Corps was training. They were all talking together, and I caught various snatches of reminiscence or discussion. This was the first of many thousands of times that I was to listen to the Flying Corps "talk shop."

It is sometimes curious to see, at some "poodle fake," a Flying Corps officer engaged in a sprightly conversation with some jolly girl or other. All will go well (I can assure the reader that a Flying Corps officer personally sees to this) until he sees another member of the corps, who probably comes over and sits down with them; three-quarters of a minute later the girl is sitting back resignedly, while the two jabber away nineteen to the dozen about aircraft and the various curious things, mechanical and human, pertaining thereto; occasionally throwing her a word so she shan't feel out in the cold, which she nevertheless always does!

This may be a social failing, but officially it is a wonderfully good thing and one sometimes learns tremendously useful tips, which the *raconteur* has probably had to pay quite dearly to learn!

All the way down the tarmac more were sitting waiting their turn to fly, or sauntering up and down. Some of these people looked very impressive. One sees a man wearing a beautiful long flying coat with an expensive fur collar, wonderful hairy gauntlets, all set off by a fur lined cap and goggles of the latest and most costly type. One feels very humble, and is apt to think that here is *the* man! The hero of a thousand battles, the dauntless stuntist, the man who can fly anything from a carrier pigeon to a Zeppelin!

But these idols generally have feet of clay, and turn out to be youngsters waiting about for their first flight.

On the other hand, when one sees a personage dad in a filthy oily flying coat hanging in tatters, with a hat which has lost all semblance or pretence of shape, one is fairly safe in saying that the man could write several books about his experiences at the Front and then not tell a lie.

Such is life!

My fellow pupils in the squadron were meanwhile either going up alone or with an instructor, so I set about examining the type of machine I was to fly in.

This was the Maurice Farman "Longhorn," so named that, because of its lack of agility in the air, the world had nicknamed it the "Mechanical Cow." This particular kind of mechanical cow possessed an elevator situated way out in front of the Nacelle or body of the machine, supported by two long outriggers. The machines with these long outriggers were called "Longhorns" and those without them, "Shorthorns."

They were only meant to be training machines, to fly slowly and control easily and steadily. Their construction was strong, as well it might be, and the tail was supported by four long tail-booms, sufficiently far apart to allow the propeller to revolve between them, as the machine was a "pusher" and not a "tractor."

Piano wire, and a great quantity of it, was used instead of galvanised cable, and this lent the machine a particularly complicated appearance, which gave rise to some bright youth's writing out the following "Rigging Instructions":

Take several truck loads of wire, pliers, and assistants, and obtain a strong and healthy canary. Place the canary in the middle of the machine. Apply wire until canary is absolutely unable to escape. The machine is then ready to fly!

The Nacelle contained the engine and tanks at the rear end and two seats at the front. The controls were duplicated in order that instruction might be carried out and mistakes rectified, etc. The height recorder, engine revolution counter, watch, and one or two instruments completed its bumble "office."

Whatever contempt seasoned pilots are able to pour on the faithful Longhorn, they nearly all have reason to be grateful to it. It provided a novice with a sort of aerial rocking horse to make his first efforts on, and considering their low power and the way they are worked and handled by muscular pupils, the machines worked remarkably well.

About 7:30 p. m. the instructor bade me, "Get in the back seat of Number 502."

I clambered up, got in, and buckled the safety belt around me. This belt is very broad-about nine inches—and very strong, designed to hold one firmly in the machine whatever happens, and has undoubtedly saved hundreds of lives, for in the event of a bad crash, if the pilot was not strapped in he would be almost certain to be thrown crushingly into the ground or engine, or whatever happened to be near. The belt is provided with a quick release which enables it to be instantly disengaged.

The pilot got into his seat in front of me and tested the controls. These consisted of a rudder bar for the feet which was wired up directly to the rudder, and an upright column on a universal joint with, affixed to the top, a cross bar with handles. To dive, the whole column is pushed forward, or with the reverse effect, pulled back, acting on the elevators at the tail of the machine, while lateral control was obtained by depressing one side or other of the cross bar, which was wired up to ailerons or flaps on the rear edge of the wing extremities.

Now came the business of starting the engine, which was always done in an absolutely stereotyped manner, so that the mechanic cannot be injured by the engine starting when he does not expect it.

"Switch off, petrol on, air closed, suck in, sir," shouted the mechanic.

"Switch off, petrol on, air closed, suck in," answered the pilot, suiting the actions to the words. The mechanic twisted the propeller, thus turning the engine and sucking the petrol vapour into the cylinders. "Contact, sir."

The pilot nearly closed the throttle and answering, "Contact," switched on the ignition.

The mechanic gave a mighty pull to the propeller, and the engine started.

The pilot ran it slowly some little time (to give it a chance to warm up) and then opened the throttle full out, watching the revolution indicator meanwhile, the machine being prevented from rushing forward by large wooden chocks placed in front of the wheels of the undercarriage. When he was satisfied that the engine was in perfect order, he throttled it down again and waved his hand over his head, the signal for "chocks away."

This having been done the engine was accelerated a little, and we taxied out across the aerodrome so as to get the longest run up wind, as a pilot always starts off facing the wind, the machine thus climbing faster over a given stretch of ground.

A man's feelings before his first flight are always mixed. Previously longing for a chance to fly, when he once gets strapped into the machine and hears the engine start, he begins to wish that he had remained safely on the ground! This is succeeded by the knowledge that one has to go through with it anyway, and he tries to pluck up what courage he can, which is usually very little! I suppose I was thinking about the same as most people as we taxied out, although I was not particularly nervous, as I implicitly trusted the pilot, who was a friend of mine.

Presently we turned into the wind and stopped for a moment, while the pilot leaned back to give me some instructions.

"Feel the controls lightly and notice what I do. Don't get nervous and grasp them heavily, because if you do exciting things might happen. Just sit steady and get used to being up."

I nodded and he turned forward and opened the throttle.

The engine now rose to a deafening roar, and the machine began to move forward, slowly at first, then faster and faster, bumping rapidly along the ground. The pressure of wind began to increase intensely, until it and the engine blended into one steady roar of sound.

The bumping suddenly ceased, and we rushed smoothly forward up a gentle sloping path, the machine feeling as steady and secure as a rock. To see the ground flashing by and falling away beneath gives a most wonderful sense of exhilaration—power—the joy of speed! One feels indeed a superman, caught up in that glorious rush through the great boundless space, while the earth with all its little petty life falls rapidly down the sands of feet below.

It all seemed so easy and secure that I stopped gaping about me and began to pay more attention to the business in hand. I had my hands and feet on the controls and I could feel the constant but very slight movements on the part of the pilot. In fact, it seemed miraculous that such small movements could control such a vast contrivance rushing along at sixty miles an hour. Every now and again one wing or the nose would give a little upward or downward bump, which the pilot instinctively countered with the slightest possible movement of the controls. We went on like this for some time, while I tried to imagine that I was flying the machine.

Presently a gust blew her nose up quite a little, and I instinctively, and instantly, pulled the control column forward to neutralise it. The pilot looked round immediately and nodded his head with a smile. I felt fearfully bucked at this and began to essay even more, trying to counteract every little movement on the part of the machine, and keep it steady.

In a minute or so the pilot took his hands off the control and waved them gently to show me that I was to try and fly the machine, but to my great relief keeping them jolly close to the handles to rectify any of my mistakes!

We went on like this for a little while while I "worked" quite a deal with the machine, making many movements which were unnecessary, with my mind extremely active.

"There's her nose coming up a bit—put it down. No, that's too much. Ah! I suppose that's about right. Is that wing falling a bit? Pull it back again Oh, damn There's the nose wrong again. Never mind, I'm flying the machine. I'M FLYING IT! (Whew! What a gust!!) I wonder if the machine is really strong enough? Suppose it must be anyway. Oh, dear, there's another machine right ahead of us." (It really was half a mile away.) "I wish he'd go down. Damn the man, what's he want to come up here for? I wonder if I can turn. Let's try a little rudder—as you were! By Gad, that didn't feel right! Let's have another try—"

Every now and again the pilot would give the controls a sharp tap to indicate what I should do or what I was overdoing. Of course all my movements were very jerky and exaggerated, and I was, so to speak, "over controlling" the machine. Then he seemed to feel my efforts to turn to the right, he nodded and put his hands on the controls.

Then things happened.

To my horror, the machine now careened wildly over on its side, while the floor seemed endeavouring to drive my feet and stomach into my head!

I let go the controls and feverishly clutched the sides of my seat, gazing fearfully down at the right wing tip vertically below me. The earth seemed whirling about in all sorts of strange mad ways, and in fact anywhere but where it ought to have been. My anxiety was about reaching bursting point when the earth slid smoothly back right under me. The floor stopped its efforts, and we were being carried quietly on again by the patient machine, which I thought very good of it!

As soon as I had collected my wits again I knew that the pilot had done a fast vertically banked turn.

Perhaps I had better explain that if a pilot tries to turn rapidly, centrifugal force throws the machine outwards on the same principle as a boy whirling a stone on a piece of string round his head. To counteract this tendency the pilot "banks" the machine until he presents the underside of his wing surface to the outside of his circle, and the machine thus being prevented from "side slipping" outwards turns in a perfect circle. The sharper the turn the more bank, and the pilot evidently considered that I needed "gingering" up!

More shocks followed as we did more turns, but by the third or fourth one I was able to look over the side with great, though be it whispered, very shallow, *sang froid*.

One of his last turns brought the aerodrome in front of us, up wind, and the roar of the engine ceased in the most uncanny manner.

I realised that we were gliding back to earth.

This glide was the most glorious sensation of all, for with the engine silent, but for the shrill whistle on the wires, one feels that it is almost flying on one's wings.

We are sweeping down quite a gentle slope, the machine responding instantly at the slightest touch of the controls. The aerodrome began to get larger and larger, and the postage stamp effect of the earth began to fade, as we dropped down.

A few more moments and the pilot shouted back, "Three hundred. Watch how I land her."

The grass grew rapidly more distinct and more distinct as we drew towards it. I began to have a horrible fear that we were going straight into the earth, when we gradually and smoothly began to alter position, the tail dropping until we were gliding quickly along, level with, and it seemed almost touching, the grass. The rush of wind died down, and I suddenly heard the undercarriage wheels spinning round.

A soft, barely felt impact, and we were rolling quietly along the ground, after a perfect landing.

"Thank you ever so much, sir. That was simply wonderful! I don't think I shall ever forget it!"

"All right, lad. I'll take you up again first thing in the morning. Now, Jones, you next. Come along. Hurry up!"

I went and sat down on the tarmac feeling fearfully happy, and absolutely unable to regard the event in any form of prosaic light.

I went back again and again over each bit of the journey. Such a marvellous journey it seemed to me.

Well! Well! The first flight is an experience never forgotten, whatever the *blasé* may say!

It was the custom of instructors to put little notices in the mess after dinner stating the names of those pupils they required for early morning flying the next day. This morning flying commenced at 5 a.m.—a time peculiarly suited for the novice, as the air is very calm and free from "bumps." Thus, more advanced pupils flew in the middle of the day, while the new ones took the early morning and also the late evening, when similar weather conditions prevail.

To my glee my name was down for 5:30 a. m., so that night I made use of a big cardboard notice which was hung outside every door, blank on one side and with "Call me" printed on the other side in large black letters, so that when the responsible officer decided that the weather was suitable for flying, the servants detailed for duty came round and wakened every occupant who advertised his need. If flying was considered impracticable, one was allowed to lie to until about 7:30.

My peaceful slumbers were broken by the local Gabriel sounding his trump in a very hoarse and early morningish—

"Five er' clock, an' e'rly flyin', sir!"

Ten minutes later I was eagerly hurrying up to the hangar, outside of which the engines were being warmed up in the cold morning breeze. One of the mechanics used to make splendid cocoa with the aid of an ingenious artifice consisting mainly of an old tin can and a blow lamp. If the method of brewing was not exactly that practised in the "Cecil," the resulting pleasure to the drinker might well have turned that august *caravanserai* green with envy! The officers paid a subscription to the brewer, in consideration of which he guaranteed the best results.

I was taken up again by the same instructor and we made a great number of landings (landing of course being the most difficult part to teach a novice). After each landing the instructor would explain to me what I should have done had I been alone, always insisting on a light touch on the controls. This last is of the greatest importance, as a man who grasps the controls as if he was trying to loop an Atlantic liner will never make a good pilot. His landings will be coarse and clumsy, no matter how much flying he does; also an instructor is in an infernally awkward predicament if a strong but unskilled pupil clutches the control tightly, thus preventing the instructor from overcoming his mistakes!

After breakfast came more flying and sometimes practice in inspecting the machines—that is to say, examining them for possible loose wires, strains, etc. There was generally some drill and an hour's lecture before lunch, after which one was free until 4 o'clock, when flying recommenced and carried on until 9. A large portion of this time I naturally spent on the ground, while other people had their turns in the air, and I saw many things which were sometimes exciting, or interesting, but at all times very humorous. The fact that scores of machines were landing, taking off, and flying round the fringe of the aerodrome demanded the enforcement of strict rules of the air, such as on which side a machine overtaking another passed, giving way to machines landing, etc.

All machines had to make either left or right hand circuits of the aerodrome according to the order of the day, which was decided by the direction of the wind. Coloured flags flown from the roofs of the hangars showed which circuit obtained, while a man was detailed to keep going a large "smudge" fire, the smoke of which showed pilots the exact direction of the wind as they landed.

With such a large crowd of novices it was only to be expected that these rules would be broken, and a solitary machine would be seen boring its frightful way round, in the opposite direction to anyone else, followed by the heartfelt curses of everyone on the ground and in the air, especially the latter. As you pass this type of machine in the air, one generally sees the pilot peering intently, into his cockpit, watching his instruments, apparently torn by desire to ascertain: (a) How much petrol there was in his tank, (b) The engine revolutions, (c) The oil pressure, (d) His speed, (e) His height. All in perfect oblivion to anything else!

One day, as I was gliding down to land, one of these gentry all but crashed into me. I just saw him coming in time and sheered off with great violence, while he drove by, his head in his "office," quite unconscious of our mutual peril!

Watching the various landings was of course the best sport of all. Some would rush down rather precipitately, hit the ground too fast, and in words of the innocent old lady, "Finish up in big hops like a little bird." If the hops were not sufficiently bird-like, the undercarriage was taken away in a sack.

Others would make most perfect landings, but unfortunately about six feet above the ground! There was usually just time to make a quick bet on the probable result before the machine "pancaked" down, and broke or did not break itself according to its youth and strength.

Some pilots stood their machines smartly up on their noses, leading to a Tower of Pisa effect, their tail flapping desolately in the breeze while they hung in their belts, moodily gazing at their fell-work.

Machines making good landings were generally found to be instructors and pupils doing dual control, or else some precocious wizard of a pupil who really flew well!

Landing a machine is darned easy when you know how and once have "got it," but, even as the Scotchman said that there were "whuskies and whuskies," so there are landings and landings! The machine can either be landed very gracefully or on the other hand brought to rest without actually breaking it. The latter is about the best to be expected from a new pupil! There is a saying that "any fool can fly, but it takes a flyer to land," which is a very true one.

One could afford to laugh at every other squadron's antics but one's own. When another squadron crashed, there was unholy glee, but one on the part of one of our own people brought forth great rage on the part of the man who was due to take the machine up next.

The most exciting thing of all, the *pièce de resistance*, so to speak, was to watch the first solos (pupils taking the machine up for the first time alone).

We could follow almost every thought that passed through an unfortunate's mind by watching his machine. The doomed man would generally taxi the machine out at a funeral pace to his starting point, turn round, and then wait a rather unnecessarily long time, which he afterwards explained as "making sure that no other machines wanted to get off in front of him." Then, taking his courage in both hands, bang open would go the throttle (much to the misery of the wretched engine, which received a fearful jolt in its stomach thereby) and the machine would violently start forward, wearing a "Now I'm in for it. Oh, Gawd!" look all over it!

The youthful god of the air would then creep carefully round and cautiously avoid any attempt at banking the machine, while the unfeeling spectators made up bets about his landing. If the direction of the wind allowed it, and the pupil had any brains at all, he made his landing as far away from the tarmac as he could, and preferably on the other side of some small swell in the ground.

If the machine would still trundle along the ground when he had landed, he would taxi proudly in and tell everyone what a magnificently judged landing he had made, over which the flight commander generally expressed a silent scepticism by minutely examining the undercarriage for damage!

Serious crashes, however, were very rare. I only saw one in which the pilot was badly hurt during the whole of my stay on the station. The general public sometimes appear to imagine that a crash is not improbable on almost every flight. To the contrary, hundreds and hundreds of flights are made successfully by pupils for every one on which a crash occurs, and even then a crash, as I have said, is not generally very bad.

Bad crashes are generally caused by some serious error of judgment too close to the ground to enable the pilot to right the machine (this height again depending on his skill). A good pilot of sure judgment can throw his machine about in the air within a few hundred feet of the ground, while an inexperienced man will make a mess of things, and perhaps get the machine in some momentarily uncontrollable position and hit the ground while he is getting it right again. For this reason "stunting" is forbidden under two or three thousand feet.

The modern aeroplane is so designed that providing the engine be throttled down, it will of its own accord right itself to its normal flying position from any position in which it can be put, without the pilot's aid. For instance, let us suppose a pilot places a machine upside down in the air, closes the throttle, and lets go of the controls. The machine's inherent stability will assert itself, its nose will drop until it is diving vertically, from which it will "flatten out" to its normal glide. Indeed, if he puts all controls central, the pilot may place the machine on its tail, wing tip, or nose, and the machine will eventually fetch up in a dive, when full control is again possible.

The only danger to avoid in ordinary flying is to mishandle the machine so that she loses flying speed. Directly an aeroplane loses this forward motion it descends from being a straining, willing, and obedient servant, to a ponderous mass, falling clumsily through the air.

But providing it has the height and is not interfered with it will in a few seconds regain flying speed and become once more obedient to the slightest touch.

A skilful pilot is able to hurl the machine about in any way that pleases him—upside down, diving, looping, etc.—and retain absolute control the whole time, but this naturally takes experience. Sometimes accidents are caused by lack of judgment while landing. A friend of mine provided a most excellent illustration of this on about my fifth evening on the aerodrome.

He was landing a Longhorn towards the sheds, but kept his engine on too long. Just as he touched the ground he apparently realised for the first time the fact that the machine was too close to the sheds to stop rolling in time.

Rather than crash into the sheds, he opened out his engine and took the machine off the ground, intending to fly over them. The distance unfortunately was just too short, and his undercarriage hit the roof of the shed with a fearful crash.

The whole of the undercarriage was scraped off like butter from bread, and the wings and body of the machine skated on over the roof. Arriving at the other side, they shot into a big telegraph pole.

The wings evidently considered this a good place to stay, for they draped themselves gracefully round the pole. The heavy body, however, had too much momentum, and it carried on alone and deposited itself and its terrified pilot with a most awful bang on the grass just behind the hangar. We all rushed around aghast, with the thought of what dreadful sight awaited us.

We were almost petrified to see the pilot stepping out of the wreckage cursing at the top of his voice! He was badly bruised and shaken, otherwise was most miraculously uninjured.

This was one of the luckiest escapes I ever saw.

By the end of the week I was becoming much more proficient and was able to fly and land a machine with gradually decreasing assistance from the instructor. My flying was not too bad, but my landings continued to be—well, if I had been alone they wouldn't have been landings, and that's all there is to it! I sometimes used to greatly irritate the instructor—just as I was about to make a dashed good (?) landing, I would feel a savage jerk, and perceive the pilot's lips moving rapidly.

He would then finish off the landing and turn round to me for a little heart-to-heart chat.

"If you want to break your —— neck, go and —— well do it alone! I want some dinner tonight! Don't pull her up about twenty feet from the floor," or "Don't try and rush into the earth as if you wanted to bore through to Hades—you will get there quite naturally."

One evening, however, to our mutual joy, it suddenly "came to me." I made an excellent landing and followed it up with about a dozen more, without the instructor having to touch the controls. After the last one the instructor turned the machine towards the hangar and we taxied in. When we finally pulled up he jumped out and turned to me.

"Righto, you're good enough now. Take this machine up solo."

With a falling heart and a dreadfully sinking sensation in the stomach, I ventured on:

"Er—er—Don't you think I had better have another landing or two!"

"Landing be dashed! You push off. Just keep cool and think what you are doing all the time. Be careful how you turn and see that there are no machines in your way when you start to land. Just make one circuit and then put her down."

With this very sensible advice buzzing in my head I dejectedly and slowly taxied out. Now, I have yet to see the pilot who did not have a little "wind up" before his first solo! One generally feels one's self incapable of ever getting the machine off the ground, and as to landing—Ugh!

One has a "never go solo today if you can put it off till tomorrow" feeling, which, the instructor being pressing, and flying inevitable, is succeeded by a last farewell look at the hangars and tarmac, and above all, the fortunates sitting on it!

With the machine turned into the wind, I gingerly opened up the throttle, then grasped the controls fiercely with both hands. I was never so concentrated before in my life, and watched the poor old Longhorn as if it had been doing three hundred miles an hour instead of its gentle fifty-five. As we got off the ground I was still rather in a confused state of mind, but soon cooled down as we were flying along in the easiest manner imaginable. I even turned and watched the hangars as they slid quickly by and downwards, and further took one hand off the control and waved it to my shed as I passed with the greatest *savoir faire* imaginable (for which I was afterwards soundly cursed by the instructor!). It was a lovely summer evening and the air was as calm as glass. No tremor or bump disturbed our course, and I felt quite happy and elated to think that I was at last a pilot.

I began to edge carefully round in a big circle (any idea of banking the machine and turning quickly made me shudder to even think of). By this time my elation was shining with a considerably dulled light, as the prospect of landing became larger and larger.

I looked down over the side at the mess, five hundred feet below, and wistfully wondered whether I should have dinner in it that night, or rather I didn't wonder very much, feeling quite positive that I should not, but instead find myself in that lonely and cordially disliked establishment embellished with a Red Cross! However, I floated on a good way down wind and then edged round again and headed home, feverishly hoping that the aerodrome would be clear of machines.

I may state here that this idea was always scouted by the efforts of the four other squadrons who possessed tractors known as the B. E. 2 C.—an official designation which was soon altered by the Flying Corps to the extraordinary name of Quirk! How this name originated I do not know but yet I might say what else could you call them?

There were always several Quirks landing, taking off, and taxiing in and out. One could always be perfectly sure when one wanted to land to find at least six of them spread about every available spot on the aerodrome, calmly sitting down with absolute unconcern to one's efforts to reach the earth again!

I had a momentary sneaking hope that they would be there so that I should have an excuse to put off my landing another circuit. However, the Fates decreed that the aerodrome should be absolutely free, and I gave up all hope. Allow me to tell the contemptuous reader that the moment before one cuts off the engine to land on one's first flight is an extraordinarily unhappy one!

I throttled down and got nicely set in my glide, eyeing the ground with a most piercing gaze. Empires might totter, wars stop, the Mauretania drive down Piccadilly like a taxi cab, but I meant to apply that machine to the ground, softly. Oh, so softly. To my astonishment, I did, making a most beautiful landing, and was congratulated by the instructor.

My hat could scarcely balance itself on my head as I walked down to mess that evening, and the burning desire of my life was for the night to pass by so that I could go and do it again. At dinner I was most casual.

"Oh, ya-as! Took a Longhorn up this evening."

"First time?"

"Oh, ya—as! There's nothing to it! The camp looks jolly fine in the sunset. Have you gone solo yet? O—hi" In accents of immeasurable superiority, knowing all the time that the poor devil hadn't.

I was up for early flying the next morning and did a great many landings. The day soon proved to be very hot and tremendously "bumpy." About 10:30 the squadron commander told me to take a machine and stay up for about two hours to gain "experience in bumps."

It certainly looked as if I should, as anyone with half an eye could not help noting how unsettled the air was. After seeing the tanks filled with petrol and oil I took her up and commenced one of the most disagreeable flights I can remember. "Bumps" are disturbances in the air due to numbers of natural causes. For instance, when a very strong sun is shining its rays warm any bare ground, such as a stubble field, which in its turn heats the air above it, the hot air rising very rapidly. Next to the stubble field there may be a wood, where trees protect the ground, which remains damp, the air above it being cold and moisture laden. This cold air descends very rapidly. As one passes from one to the other the whole machine gets a very sharp bump—in fact, it feels as if some great invisible hand had smacked the machine.

There are also gusts, heat eddies, sharp upward currents—in fact quite a number of disturbances which tend to throw the machine about. This means, in a slow machine, a great deal of work controlling; a fast aeroplane will cut through bumps and the only feeling to them is a little flick of the wings, whereas on slow machines, one may drop one or two hundred feet in one "bump" or rise the same height. This sort of thing being unexpected and violent, is not frightfully pleasant, the motion being almost as bad as that of a Ford car going full speed along a much be-shelled road! Well, to say that is, I suppose, a great exaggeration, for Dante should have visualised Fords on shelled roads in his *Inferno!*

By the end of an hour my wrists were very tired and my interior economy a trifle "seedy." I had got over wondering whether the machine could stand the "bumps" as it had stood them for an hour and no port of it was apparently missing, although after some specially militant efforts on the part of the air I felt a species of mild surprise at seeing the two wings stretching their two faithful selves on either side of me. The moment that the dashboard watch indicated my time was up, I flopped down with a sigh of relief and taxied in. My wrists were nearly numbed and I had quite a "Yo, ho, my hearty!" sort of walk. It was splendid experience and flying the machine in calm weather seemed so simple that one wondered why they ever took the trouble for hours, to teach people how to fly. I flew this type of machine quite a lot for another three or four days, and was then, to my great delight, transferred to another squadron to be trained as a scout pilot.

I was absolutely overjoyed at this, for it is the ambition of every embryo pilot to fly the fast little scouts.

Having thanked my instructors very much I proceeded to report immediately to my new squadron, where I was soon given my first dual control flight on a much more sensitive machine, which was also equipped with the standard controls; that is, a rudder bar and a stick mounted on a universal joint. The two are used in conjunction with each other; for instance, to turn, rudder is applied and the stick pushed over towards the inside of the turn; whichever way the stick is moved the machine follows—push the stick forward, the machine dives—pull it back, she climbs—put it over to one side of the other, and the machine banks accordingly.

The new machine was quite different from the other type and was very delicate on its controls, to which it would instantly respond at the slightest touch. The Longhorn had seemed quite delicate at first, but with increasing experience I soon realised that it was a rather heavy handed affair. The new machine descended at a much steeper angle, and this, combined with the light touch necessary, made one feel all at sea. For the first few minutes that I felt the controls and tried to fly her I thought that I should never be able to. When we came down again the instructor gave me a little lecture on "light hands."

> Just like a horse with a delicate mouth, feel it gently and never pull. Just use your fingers, not your fists. Don't worry about your head, your eyes, and your judgment—that will all come. If you have only got 'light hands' I know I can make a good scout pilot out of you. Just think that you want to bank your machine round and you will find yourself squeezing the stick just enough. Don't wag the stick about all over the place. If you do you will never be a pilot.

I took this advice very much to heart, to a marked improvement in my flying. I found the instructor's words no exaggeration. For instance, the slightest touch was sufficient to swing her right over in the desired direction. I was taught how to get the tail up and keep the machine straight taking off, and the exact moment to put the tail down in landing, etc.

The next evening I was sent up solo—another wind-up proceeding. I made an excellent landing and was immediately sent off to do a lot more. The next day I had a very lively time in somewhat "bumpy" weather, the machine's large wings and delicate control rendering it peculiarly susceptible to any unpleasantness in this nature. The same evening the squadron commander came up and asked me "How many hours I had done?" I told him.

He eyed me for a moment, then said: "Take number 800 up and do ten landings, then report to me and I'll start you off on a war machine." I carried out "the ten landings without breaking anything. I sought him out about 7 o'clock in his office, and he queried: "How do you like those machines you have been flying?"

"Very well, sir!"

"Land them all right, eh?"

"Haven't actually smashed one yet, sir!"

"Have you ever had a crash yet?"

"No, sir!" Very proudly.

"Umph. You'll probably be a damn sight better pilot when you have; have you tried to stunt them yet?"

"Not much, sir."

"Umph! Well, as a matter of fact, I've watched your flying and it's not too bad, now

I'll take you up on the—— and play about with it and do some landings for you to see how it's done. There isn't any dual control, but they are quite easy to handle. I just want you to notice how I do it and then you'll find no difficulty when you try. The main thing is to manage your engine properly; this is a war machine and considerably more powerful than the ones you have been flying, but there's no reason to get excited about that. Another thing; while I don't want you to try and stunt about with it in your first few flights, before you go overseas you must be able to do almost anything with a machine. I'll do one or two mild stunts this evening for you to see how they are done."

Then we left his office and got in the machine. I felt very pleased to be in a real war machine—the sort they had been using in France. It had a hundred horse power engine and was in every way better, but was of course not a patch on the scouts.

The squadron commander was a very cheerful fellow and a splendid pilot. After testing the engine we started off, and the feeling of power and the rate of climb seemed splendid, and as I only had to sit and admire things in general, I was enjoying myself immensely.

We soon got up to what I judged to be about three thousand feet. After a few minutes' steady flying I felt the machine suddenly dip, and we began to gather a lot of extra speed. I was still peacefully surveying the world underneath and not paying much attention to the machine, when, without any warning, the machine's nose swung violently upright until we seemed to be standing bolt upright on our tail! While I was still gasping at this, we swished right over on one side and simply crashed through the air for about five hundred feet. I was by this time clutching the sides and feeling tremendously pious. I cannot say my past life passed before me—I was too frightened! But I had a distinctly "If I get out alive I'll be very good in future" feeling.

While still engaged in these not very cheerful soliloquies, the earth, which for the past few seconds had unaccountably disappeared, appeared again, strange to say, underneath us, to my great joy. My happiness was short lived, for immediately it climbed up and looked at me right along the surface of the wing, while we spun violently around until I was too dizzy to think. After a seeming eternity the spinning stopped and we came level again. Then the engine stopped, but the nose still remained well up instead of us gliding as usual. I had just begun to turn round to see what was the matter, when the whole machine dropped away from me like a stone.

I came up violently against the safety belt, which yanked me back on my seat with a dull thud, which I felt but could not hear. We were then pointing vertically in the most sickening dive imaginable. The hum of the wires rose to a piercing scream. The whole machine shuddered with the strain, and I had a vague remembrance of having left my stomach quite a thousand feet above me! I stared at the ground below me and made rapid calculations on what we should look like when the ambulance found us. I mused, "Now the ambulance will come through *that* gate and go straight across the field. We shall be close by *that* big tree—"

But slowly and surely up came the nose until we were once again level. I felt a sharp kick in my back from the pilot, and looked round to see him grinning with huge delight at me. I responded with a very wan smile. My feelings were past description. The pilot then landed and took off again about six times, and then returned to the shed.

Having stopped the engine, he leaned over and asked:

"Did you like that?"

"Yes—s, sir!"

"Well you see how she can be thrown about (Heavens, I did!) and how to land her. Keep your engine switched off until you have finished your landing. You'll find she's very easy to fly. Don't let your speed drop below seventy, but bring her down at about sixty. Now don't feel nervous—machine will almost fly itself. Would you like me to do a few more stunts to get you used to her?"

"Oh, no, sir!" very hurriedly!

I then got in his seat and he explained the engine controls, after which I started off. The machine flew me off the ground with great care. I had very little to say in the matter. I held the stick and felt clever but the machine really did it all. My landing was rather of the "hopping like a little bird" type, but I got down safely, which was after all my only object. After this I started down to mess for a drink, not being quite sure whether to be very elated or rather thoughtful.

Stunting, after all, is an acquired taste!

Chapter 3

Overseas

It was at this point in my career that I first began to take a serious interest in that most peculiar, interesting, and at all times (except to the pilot) humorous instrument, an aero engine.

Young pilots, in the first rosy flush of their Flying Corps experience, become obsessed with the altogether mad notion that these shiny, complicated, and noisy objects are capable, not to say willing, to support them in the air as long as they (the pilots) wish to remain there. With further, usually sad bitter experience, there comes disillusion, and eventually one is able to classify engines into three main classes.

First, engines that are quite honest about it, and resist all efforts to obtain the slightest sign of life from them.

Second, aero engines, which employ guileful camouflage, starting off well, luring their unhappy human freight just out of the aerodrome, and carefully choosing their spot so that the pilot is confronted with houses, back gardens, barbed wire, and a canal or two, immediately stop.

Third, engines which go constantly and keep on going until there is no more petrol.

The first has done its bit towards the war by necessitating a large increase of his clerical staff, accompanied by the introduction of adding machines and other labour saving devices, on the part of the Recording Angel; most frequently caused by the expert and sulphurous profanity of the unfortunate air mechanics and flight sergeants doomed to look after them. The lunatic asylums can alone tell the dark and dreadful tale of devastation they have wrought in humanity! The second is perhaps the most fiendish of all. Even experienced and disillusioned pilots, possessors of old and oily flying coats, are caught by them. The breed will burst into full song at the first touch from the mechanic, and use every means in its power to entice the miserable beings sitting behind it off the ground. Having once got them there, fully at its mercy, it, as I have said, selects that part of the surrounding country possessing the hardest and most sharp pointed obstacles, and dives into them, eventually ending its days in old scrap iron barrels in the Whitechapel Road. Apart from military funerals, it may also be said to be responsible for quite a number of marriages between crippled flying officers and young society nurses!

The third type, if existent at all, is only known to great personages, wearing many swords and stars, and is probably maintained in a case of the finest Bohemian glass and concealed in the Bank of England, and there jealously guarded by specially selected fierce and bloody soldiery.

Thus it will be seen that engines are by no means what they are popularly supposed to be! In the course of time, and with the help of beneficent Providence, a man may eventually learn to circumvent their malevolent efforts and force them to perform about half the performance their optimistic and altogether sanguine inventor prophesied they would. About tea time one fine day I was sent off, well primed with maps, to do my first cross country flight.

Having climbed to about four thousand feet the engine going like a clock, I set off, picking my way from landmark to landmark and comparing the printed map with the real one beneath me I was very anxious to hit off my destination some sixty miles away, and followed my progress over the country with most minute care, like an aerial sleuth. I was enjoying myself quite a lot, the engine running perfectly—a beautiful afternoon and above all, I knew where I was!

After about fifty minutes of very pleasant flying, I arrived over the aerodrome which was my destination. I executed a steep spiral (which I should not have dared to do over my own aerodrome, where I should have been recognised) and made my landing. It seemed to me by this time to be getting pretty dark, and as I had by hearsay already grasped the excellent notion that cross country journeys should be taken coolly and not with any rash attempts to hurry, I had the machine put up for the night. (This thesis, by the way, was not exactly popular with commanding officers.) My hosts dined me very well! Have no fear, not too well!

At 6 a. m. the next morning, with myself full of coffee and the tanks full of petrol, the machine and I again took to the Empyrean. I climbed fairly high once more, as the first twenty miles of my journey lay over very nasty country—small fields, big trees, and so forth. It was a most beautiful, cold, but calm morning, and I soon left the aerodrome behind me as I bowled peacefully along at a good round seventy miles an hour.

I was now over about the worst bit of country I had to cover; I tried to not look at it, but instead gazed hopefully ahead to where I knew the good kind commenced. Then it was that the engine came into its own.

Having carefully bided its time, it selected the worst bit of country it could find, and uttering an ear-splitting grating bang, stopped dead.

I accordingly started to glide, hunting wildly round for some safe spot to perch. The only place offering any attractions was a very small field having a farmhouse at one end, a railway embankment on one side and a wood on the other. The remaining side, however, was open, and as luck would have it, this was the direction I had to follow in order to land against the wind. All the remaining country seemed to be under standing corn.

I rapidly got lower and lower and flashed by my field going down wind. The question now was precisely when to turn round so as not to over shoot or under shoot the mark. I waited until what I thought to be the right moment then decided to turn. I was then about ninety feet from the ground.

We "hurrooshed" round with the most alarming bank, straightened out, and landed just right

I stepped out of the machine feeling a devil of a fellow, and began to examine the engine. Save for the fact that it rattled dismally when I turned it I didn't gather much information. The first representative of the civil population then appeared, in the shape of a small boy eating an apple, who enquired if I was an airman. I blushingly admitted the fact, but he looked at me rather doubtfully. He probably thought I had been dropped by Santa Claus! Two mounted soldiers then appeared, galloping towards me, through corn, hedges or whatever else had the misfortune to be in their way, and pulled up and dropped from their panting horses. They seemed disappointed to see me and the machine apparently intact, stating rather in injured tones that they had "seen the machine disappear behind the railway embankment all up on one side." Telling them that I was sorry to have disappointed them I despatched one back for a guard. This soon appeared (from a big cavalry depot nearby) together with the commanding officer's horse, compliments, and invitation to breakfast, all of which I took.

Before breakfast I rang up my aerodrome over long distance phone and asked for a fresh engine to be sent down in a car. I spent a peaceful day while the fresh engine was being brought down, and subsequently fitted. About 5 o'clock the mechanics reported all O. K., and I "hoicked" the machine out of the small field. As the new engine ran very well I thought it would be a good thing to show my kind hosts, the cavalry officers, a little flying. I accordingly executed a few mild stunts, when, just as I was on the middle of one, the engine, with all the guile of its hateful species, began to splutter. It spluttered more every second, so I turned hurriedly and made back for my field.

I switched off and tried to land, but was too close. I touched ground at about seventy, and rather than make a certain crash, switched on again and tried to fly off. The engine carried me on from my good field to the middle of a large area of standing corn and then stopped again. I was only two feet or so above it and there was no time to do anything, so the corn caught the undercarriage and we turned two smart somersaults. I had a vision of broken struts and pieces of fabric flying through the air, and we finally ground ourselves well into the earth. Strange to say, I was absolutely uninjured, and unbuckling the belt rose like a Phoenix from the wreck!

The next morning a little procession entered my aerodrome, consisting of myself leading the way in a small car, followed by two huge lorries piled with wreckage.

Such was my first crash!

Of course I blamed it on the engine, but, be it whispered, this might not have been altogether true. There were a good few things in engine management that I had yet to learn.

For all the hard things I have said about engines, I really admire the species very much. Built of the lightest steel, with cylinders, pistons, and all its various mechanism so light and so apparently frail; working at all altitudes and in all weathers, throbbing madly round, turning the great propeller, granting sight to the eyes of the army; to be suddenly switched off while the machine twists and dives in aerial combat, then to start again, obedient to the pilot's slightest wish, and patiently exert its giant strength, perhaps hour after hour, carrying over hostile territory its freight of human lives—on whose efficiency may depend the lives of a thousand men three miles below them—to safety. Such is the modern aero-engine.

Late in the evening I was introduced to a scout by the squadron commander.

When I was installed in it he came and leaned over the side to give me, as usual, the last few words of advice.

Now don't think that because this machine is a scout, that it needs superhuman skill to fly it You will find it just like any other machine except it is very light indeed on the controls. Think what you're doing all the time. Bring her down at about seventy-five and don't forget that she has a very fine gliding angle, which means that you must switch off in plenty of time. Now don't be nervous—you're going to fly her splendidly.

I had the same feeling about taking this scout up that I did my first solo. It looked so small and powerful; but still, I thought to myself, if ever I am going to fly a scout, this is the time, so here goes! On the machines I had previously flown, there had always been time to open up the engine and then turn one's attention to taking the machine off. On this occasion, by the time I had the engine throttle properly open, we were ten feet off the ground; I involuntarily made a slight movement with the stick, but the machine made such a lightning response that I desisted and practically let the machine fly itself. To move the stick felt as though one was moving a stick of rubber instead of wood, so quickly did the machine give to it and alter position. I was by this time holding the control with my thumb and forefinger and was beginning to feel the machine better. We seemed to be climbing at an extraordinary rate, for the altimeter dial showed a thousand feet in what seemed a half minute (in reality it was fifty seconds). I began to wonder how the devil much higher I should get by the time I had completed the circle of the aerodrome.

I felt happier with the machine every minute, it was so delightful to fly. I could feel the terrific pull of the engine, and the tremendous buoyancy of the whole aeroplane. At the merest touch of her controls she flitted round to the new course—Oh! so different from the ponderous Longhorn! In fact, I was flying her so easily and well that I thought myself very big beer indeed. We were four thousand when I switched off, and I thought that, early as I had cut off the power, I should over shoot the mark. As luck would have it I placed myself just about right. We shot along the ground at a terrific pace, but the little scout was under such perfect control that there was no difficulty about it, and she allowed herself to be landed with almost—er, shall I say it?—*éclat!*

The next morning the sky was rather cloudy, so the squadron commander told me to take the scout and climb up through a gap "to get used to it."

As I climbed nearer and nearer the clouds I picked a good big gap with the blue sky showing through it, and continued to climb in large circles up through this hole. In another two minutes the clouds were hundreds of feet below me and I was gasping at the most wonderful sight I had ever seen.

Far away to the ends of space there stretched a wonderful, living sea of brilliant white cotton wool, here and there were great waves in the sea, holding deep blue shadows of mystery in their depths, up until the crest began to reflect and transmute each ray of sun into glorious purity of snowy white and colour. They looked so calm—so gentle—so friendly. They seemed to invite one to cast oneself upon their spreading couch, to be so secure and restful—to forget—to dream.

Then a patch of dull brown prosaic earth, with its tiny doll houses and toy roads, would appear indistinctly and disappear again. The spell was broken!

The pressure of my finger on the switch, the almost drowsy hum of wires, and we dropped slowly earthwards. Then a dive, charging through a damp grey fog; a momentary impression of tremendous speed, and I had exchanged the sunlit blue heavens for the dull grey underworld beneath the clouds.

I crammed in a great deal of scout flying in the next week and put in a deal of stunting practice. The squadron commander would happen along and order me to;

Go up to about eight thousand and chuck her about. Don't come down till you have done a loop, and if you do it nicely, try a spinning nose dive.

I didn't think there was any danger of me doing either of them at all, much less nicely; but nevertheless sought the chilly climes which obtained at about nine thousand with all the rapidity with which the scout would take me there, and started to do wild split-air evolutions.

After a while I plucked up what I call my courage and did what I imagined to be some quite violent aerobatics; I say what I imagine to be, for generally when one does what one thinks is a devil of a stunt turn, onlooking pilots ask "why don't you bank the machine decently, instead of making flat wide turns!"

Now I began to think about the serious business of a loop. In the old days before the war a pilot only had to perform this simple aerobatic to become famous, and become the object of the languishing hearts and glances of half the charming girls in London.

Oh! Oh! Oh! For the good old times!

The thing to do was to affect pink spotted socks and an elephantine car of unknown power, and, having by some means got one's photograph into the *Daily Mirror*, take the car grunting and roaring its odoriferous way up and down Piccadilly, hatless, in order that the damsels might see one's glossy stream lined hair!

One then invited a select party of the said damsels to the aerodrome one usually attempted to aviate over.

Having successfully or otherwise parted the undercarriage with the earth before the nearly swooning audience, a few mild stunts were attempted, inevitably resulting in a grinding crash in the sewage farm or some other popular resort. Then one returned (sometimes) by road, to the accompaniment of, "Oh! How *beautiful!* What a nerve you must have!" etc., etc.

One had—but in a different sense!

But to return to looping: having made a mental will and calculated which field I should be picked up in, I shoved the nose down to get extra speed, I pulled the stick back into my "tummy," and, crouching abjectly in my seat, awaited developments.

These followed with remarkable rapidity. I quickly realised that the great thing in looping is to get the machine back to some position which one can recognise. I made several praiseworthy attempts to locate the earth, but it unfortunately appeared to be "absent from parade" that afternoon. How and whither we went I don't know, but it was always infernally quick. Having pushed and pulled everything about the machine which would move, I let go, upon which the machine immediately righted itself and flew on with, I could have sworn, a pained look!

I need not state whether or not I tried a spinning nose dive!

At the end of the week the squadron commander said that he would recommend me for my "wings." These wings are the coveted pilot's badge, consisting of two outspreading wings, with a crown and laurel wreath in the centre, on which is embroidered "Royal Flying Corps." It is made in black and white silk and worn on the left breast of the tunic and the wearer is from then graded as a flying officer, and is eligible for duty overseas. Highly delighted by this, I hurried down to my quarters and sent my servant with two of my tunics down to the tailor's to have wings sewn on them, so that when the announcement should be published, I could blossom forth without an instant's delay!

Four o'clock next day station orders were posted up and then I was gazetted as a flying officer.

At one and a half minutes past four I strolled nonchalantly into the mess.

I wasn't noticed!

Hades!

About half an hour later, however, I was spied, and then it was a case of drinks all round.

I proceeded on leave next morning, and was as usual recalled. I had been at home exactly ninety minutes when a telegram arrived ordering me back.

What wags they were!

I reported back in quite an excited state to find that no one apparently knew why I had returned! I had just made up my mind to start back home again, when orders to embark thirty-six hours later, with three other officers, were given me.

We went to London and settled down to the business of putting the wind up its inhabitants for the evening. The next morning, this having been most successfully accomplished, and our accounts with our banker., reduced to overdrafts, we departed in the best of spirits, for, in words of the stately War Office, "Flying Duty Overseas."

Chapter 4
France

Driven by her throbbing muffled turbines, the long black ship ploughed on into the darkening grey ocean away to the southeast. On board her were crowds of all ranks of the British Army destined for the Greatest of all Adventures—infantrymen, gunners, sappers, air mechanics, chaplains, and miners—brigadiers and privates—they all stood about together on her decks. Behind them in receding England, lay everything, perhaps; all they held dear—their women-kind—children—homes—happiness. For a few months or ——?

"Ah," one might say, "they are standing gazing mournfully at dimming England—soon to be but a memory. They will be sad and thoughtful!"

But not they!

A cheery, laughing crowd—a smile on every face; much bartering of badinage and fags; much uproarious hilarity at the lifebelts the ever thoughtful Admiralty had provided; much disrespectful surmise on the eternal destination of the "All Highest;" much speculation about the girls in France!

In fact it was more like a Bank Holiday pleasure steamer!

But stay—there are some faces which are—well, thoughtful. These faces are being held carefully over the sides by their owners, who, be it whispered, had not quite yet got their sea legs—or stomachs!

It seems rather funny; we feel we ought to be standing with a "Napoleon at Elba" look, sternly facing our doom, gazing back at England in strength and silence—instead of which we seem quite happy!

I wonder if the methodical Boche would be the same?

The Isle of Wight looked very beautiful as we left it, its hills silhouetted against the sunset; I knew it very well, and my mater was at the time living there.

We smoked and talked and talked and smoked well into the night. About midnight we arrived outside Havre. Hundreds upon hundreds of twinkling lights advertised an evident hustle and business on shore, combined with contempt of the ubiquitous *Unterseeboote*. Our crossing, like thousands upon thousands of others, had been rendered perfectly safe from these gentry by the British Navy.

At about this time I dozed off to sleep in a comfortable corner of the deck. When I awoke it was 4:30 a. m. and we were steaming rapidly up a broad river. On either bank were queer little white houses, nearly covered with advertisements or in a good many cases, advertising themselves to be "*estaminets*." None of the inhabitants seemed to be stirring at such an early hour, which combined with the morning mists, gave the country a very forlorn, lonely sort of look.

Later on in the morning we moored at Rouen and soon after, under the *ægis* of the military landing officer, we were on the soil of France.

We went with the squadron commander to the Hotel D'Angleterre for breakfast. None of us had been in France before, also our French was mainly conspicuous by its absence, so we left the ordering to him, upon which he caused a profound impression amongst us by issuing a long string of orders to the *garçon*, who, more impressive still, appeared to understand him!

We were for a short while in Rouen, and stayed at one of the nicest hotels I have ever been in, the Hotel de la Poste in the Rue Jeanne D'Arc. In Rouen, of course, everything seems connected with or commemorates some part of the life of the saint. We visited the Tour Jeanne D'Arc, where she was imprisoned, the Grande Place in front of the Hotel de Ville, where she was executed, and the splendid cathedral.

Altogether we had a very interesting time in Rouen to remember when we left the next day in the squadron commander's car and headed northeast for the Front.

The journey presented a series of new objects of interest every hour. We were driving through very pretty country, over good roads, which stretched mile after mile with scarcely ever a twist in them. Occasionally an old man, or some women and children, would wave their hands to us, very cheerily, but we never saw any young men.

As the day wore on we crossed the River Somme, flowing peacefully on through scenes of the utmost rest and placidity. It almost baffled the imagination to realise that a comparatively short distance away its waters were literally crimson with the life blood of thousands of French, British, and German men, for nowhere about could be seen any signs of war, but only a calm countryside.

The inhabitants themselves were all going cheerfully about their various occasions, and from their aspect such a thing as a war might not have been existent. At the local hotel in the little village close by, *Madame la Propriétaire* cooked us a number of perfect omelets, and cracked jokes by the dozen with the squadron commander. As we went out, she stood at the door laughingly wishing us a safe journey.

The squadron commander, the last to leave, asked her a question.

For a moment her face showed the burden of those who have to stay at home and wait.

"*Oui, M'sieu, mon mari—mon fils—ils sont dans le trenchée devant Verdun, M'sieu!*"

Then she would cast the shadow from her face and merrily send us on our way as happy as she could make us, with a ringing "*Bon voyage, Messieurs! Bon voyage!*" Wonderful France!

As we ran on nearer the Front we began to pass camps of increasing size and the country became alive with French *poilus*. Mile after mile of cantonments, stores, galvanised iron huts, motor transport parks, horse and mule depots, aerodromes—men working in their camps—men marching along our road—horses being fed—horses pulling guns—long columns of hurrying ammunition trucks—long lines of them parked before the stores being loaded up with the army's food—aeroplanes in crates—aeroplanes in the air.

All the hurrying, bustling, striving—but yet the Pomp of War.

The German Chancellor's "Crushed and beaten France!" Crushed and beaten by the ceaseless pounding of her great columns of motor trucks, by the recoil of her thousands of mighty guns; by the feet of a million of her brave soldiers as they marched eastward, ready—even eager—to be "crushed and beaten" as they hurled the enemy back on the Somme, in Champagne, and most glorious of all, before their stricken city of Verdun. So this great, thriving, pulsing country was the stricken nation seen by the Germans! Oh, the fools! The fools!

We sat quite silent in the car as we watched these changing scenes, and then the whole scene changed so abruptly that we rubbed our eyes!

For we were in England; it *must* be England! The whole country, instead of being alive with *poilus*, was alive with the khaki clad members of the British Army. The motor cars, trucks, the boxes of stores,

British! British men, British horses, British guns, even British towns of galvanised iron.

No, it isn't England; only the southern end of the British Western Front! For my part, I was utterly unable to grasp—what adjective can I use?—the gigantic organisation behind the lines. Enormous towns of wood and concrete, immense hospitals. They were staggering—that is the only word for it; our loving Friend—the All Highest—would have been distinctly peeved, methinks, had he been along with us in the car!

About 6:30 we arrived at our aerodrome, which was situated in quite a peaceful spot about twelve miles from the lines. It was just sunset. A number of small, grey-bodied, powerful scouts stood near the hangars, being looked over by their mechanics after the day's work. One or two little parties of French people, in sober black, wended their way towards the village, away from whence the warm evening hour carried the soft chimes from the village church.

As we stood we looked down the long poplar hedged straight road running due east, a storm of evil looking black puffs began to dot the sky, around a barely seen speck: the work of a German anti-aircraft battery.

And to our ears came a sullen, insistent mutter; a mutter which never ceased.

CHAPTER 5

Over the Lines

Ten thousand feet below lay the aerodrome, its hangars almost indistinguishable, and the landing ground appearing so tiny that it seemed impossible that machines could ever land in it. Not a stone's throw from it, as it were, lay the village, a little mass of dark, reddish, Lilliputian houses, set round a brilliant white blob—its beautiful church. Farther afield there was spread out a wonderful living map of incredible size.

Everywhere, cut up into little tiny fields, black fields, brown fields, meadow and plough, wheat and stubble, intersected by tiny black lines—hedges. Now and again would come a wood, appearing as an almost blackish green blot on the otherwise earthy brown world.

The day was perfect, a clear blue sky and brilliant sunshine, which rendered objects uncannily distinct even from the great height; little streams winding their devious way across the broad surface of the earth gleamed like streaks of polished silver; the white, black edged ribbons that represented roads cut the country into great blocks, roads which appeared to run absolutely straight for immeasurable distances.

Naturally no living thing was discernible from my high level. I had been sent up alone to generally spy out and get used to the country. Strapped on to either knee I had maps, and I minutely compared them with the actuality beneath me, learning the country off bit by bit as I went along. I was heading eastward and bound for the lines.

After flying some time I passed over a big town, which the map showed to be Bethune. About six or seven miles east of it lay that "undiscovered country" the very name of which kindles a hundred flames of imagination; the country I had read and heard so many and such thrilling accounts of—The Lines! By these same accounts I knew of the thousand and one activities which must have been taking place beneath me. Of battalions and battalions of men in the Front line and in the reserve—of batteries of artillery—trench mortars—bombs—rifles—bayonets—snipers—observation posts—of all the paraphernalia used by friend and foe engaged in their ceaseless year in and year out struggle—of the two strings of tense, alert enemies—Teuton and Briton. What the newspapers called "The Great Band of Steel across France"—the scene of the most colossal and bloody fighting the world had ever known—but yet how different to the eyes of the airman.

Creeping down from the dim distance, shrouded in brown haze, in the north, right across the earth to the southern horizon, crept a belt of light brown, churned up, tortured nature. No sign of life could be seen, but yet all around it there seemed to lurk the most oppressive sense of brooding malignancy.

Set in the middle of the belt, close to and facing each other, were two continuous irregularly formed black threads. From them, at right angles, ran other, but very zigzag threads, until they joined a second line parallel to the first; from here struggled a maze of more and yet more threads, crawling in all directions. All over and near the trenches were millions of black spots with lightish rims,—shell holes. In places—particularly between the two opposing front lines—lay enormous craters, light yellow in colour; these were mines. No trees or fields or hedges made the country recognisable. The very roads, as they came into the belt, merged off and became lost in it. Woods had long since been blown up by roots, farmhouses reduced to holes in the ground, streams dammed up.

Yet of all the endeavour that had caused these things, no sign was visible, except that in one or two particular places I could observe little puffs of smoke spring into being and drift slowly down wind. The men who fired the shells, and those who suffered under them, were equally shrouded in mystery.

A mile or so from the belt, on either side, the country looked perfectly normal.

I felt as though I was sitting high up in the gallery of a vast theatre, waiting for a play—a play which never began.

So this was war!

I flew up and down parallel to the lines for a long time and gazed at the extraordinary panorama, which, once seen, is never forgotten: seen from the air it seems so unreal. One expects conflict and noise and shells, and blood, but instead, there lay that cold, interminable brown scar.

If I had been lonely, now I did not have far to go for company, for in front, mainly east of the lines, flew innumerable aircraft, always in little companies, or formations, as they are called, their planes glinting brilliant in the sunshine every time they turned. Some were much lower than me, others on about the same level, and then, high as I was, far above me, so far indeed that they were mere specks. Some of them hung about over a certain locality; they were probably controlling artillery fire; others flew aimlessly about in little flocks—offensive patrols looking for Huns while occasionally a large formation would sweep up behind me, cross the lines, and fly steadily on into the enemy's country—a bombing raid.

Nearly all were attended by innumerable vicious black bursts—bursting shrapnel from the energetic Teuton guns below. The shells chased the machines relentlessly, sometimes bursting so close that I expected to see the targets crumple up and fall into pieces. But yet the machines flew on uninjured. The bombing raid was met with a perfect storm of shells, and the sky around the machines took on the most curious aspect, like a sheet of blue paper over which there had been sprinkled thousands of blots of ink! Fresh formations continually crossed over, going east, while others came in on their way home with their jobs completed.

As far as I could see up and down and behind the lines was a mass of aircraft; even when distance rendered them nearly invisible, black shell bursts still advertised them to be there. I was startled by the extraordinary number of machines in the sky, for I had never seen such a quantity of aircraft before, and felt very much taken aback by the magnitude of the operations. All the machines seemed to be proceeding on their way with a businesslike sort of appearance, and it did not take a great effort of imagination to conjecture that the pilots all knew exactly what they were to do, and how to do it!

The whole scene formed a marvellous picture the Flying Corps "getting down to it" in its shirt sleeves, so to speak!

As time was getting on I remembered my orders to fly down that length of the Front over which we should thenceforward work and I therefore turned south and took stock of the lines as I went. Bethune, as I have said, lies some five or six miles from the lines. The town can be seen from a great distance as it has a good identifying feature in the shape of a rectangular reservoir on its eastern side. The La Bassée Canal runs through the town and on, by the trenches, to the shattered village of La Bassée, which is situated just within the German side. I noticed that the water on the canal looked a very dirty colour where it ran through the trench system.

South from La Bassée, the line curved out in a great sweep—the famous Loos salient. The salient consists of a tremendous network of trenches, the rearmost of which were at one time the German's front line, and a few partially blasted townlets, principal among which is Loos itself, a small mining village which was the centre of particularly bloody fighting in nineteen-sixteen.

The salient possesses a hundred points of great interest, but as they have already been dealt with at other times I will pass them by. It is sufficient to say that this great bulge in the line looks very impressive, and a great achievement on the part of the gallant troops who created it.

From the easternmost point of the salient the line sweeps back around another mining town, nearly as large as Bethune, in the shape of Lens. Some way back on our side of the line is a curious, regularly shaped collection of straight streets of battered red cottages—Noeux-le-Mines—which lies north of a large wood called the Bois de Dames. Passing Lens the line runs down for a short while with no particularly outstanding feature, until Vimy Ridge, which was even at this time a very lively spot. Passing over Vimy I came to Arras, which seemed very extraordinarily close the lines; so close that I registered an intention never to go in it on the ground!

I turned north again over Arras and went back again over the same lines, familiarising myself with every mile of it. On my way I had noticed a little distance on either side of the line, two widely spaced rows of humorous looking objects resembling that nauseating brand of *delicatessen* so dear to the Teutonic heart, the fat type of German sausage!

These were kite balloons.

The Hun balloons sat close to the ground, very wisely deeming discretion the better part of valour, but our own were about four thousand feet up. I determined to make a closer inspection, so selected one which was hanging over the Bois de Dames, and switched off, gliding down to him, and commenced a rapid circle round the balloon.

A fine cable ran from it towards the ground, and suspended from the balloon was a casket from which gesticulated its apparently infuriated occupant.

I thought at first that he was waving his hand to me, but on drawing closer I saw he was shaking his fist.

I felt rather hurt by his lack of hospitality and began to circle even closer round and round him.

In a few seconds, by which time I imagined him to be foaming at the mouth, he delved into the recesses of his mysterious basket and produced a gun, upon which I fled with all the speed I could get out of the scout!

More experience at the Front and a little common sense soon told me why he didn't love me. Imagine a man suspended in a basket, several thousand feet from the floor, by a painfully thin steel rope, in a strong westerly wind, the said basket swaying in a most agitating manner, sufficient to make even an *Ancient Mariner* liverish; give the man an extremely difficult piece of artillery observation, requiring all his attention. On the top of all this think of his feelings when a nasty, beastly aeroplane comes split-airing around him, and particularly his faithful wire rope! Even when it is apparently a British machine he wonders whether it really is, knowing full well how easily he could be set on fire.

Can you wonder that they prefer solitude?

I have a great admiration for the Kite Balloon Corps, and have known numberless cases of great bravery on the part of its personnel.

If the winch is hit—and they are continually shot at—the observer is confronted with instantly getting hold of his confidential papers, so that the Hun may not find them when the balloon eventually comes to earth, and then jumping off into about four thousand feet of space with a comic umbrella strapped to him. Despite the fact that parachutes are remarkably efficient in their working, I cannot say that I would like to do this sort of thing for a bet! How awkward it would be, for instance, to be set down violently on a spiked weather cock, and be impaled thereon, to hang and be potted by snipers!

I remember a case where the driver of the truck on which the "winch" rests driving it up and down a piece of road for six hours, dodging the shells of a German battery which was "searching" for him. The balloon being on the other end of the string, his radius of movement was naturally confined, but nevertheless he enabled the observer to do invaluable work and then be reeled in safely at the end of it, after six hours' hide and seek with shells!

Just an instance.

On my way home I bethought myself that no machine had I seen with the enemy iron cross painted on its planes, but only with our own red, white and blue ring, and wondered afresh that people yapped about our losing aerial supremacy! Feeling that I might do something to help the war on, I came down to three thousand and loosed off four drums from the Lewis gun at the German second line trenches, hopefully wishing each bullet a resting place in some fat Hun.

Just after this little show of temper, one of our big two-seaters rushed up to me, its observer brandishing his machine gun in my direction. Much alarmed, I swung the machine over to show my markings and at the same time brandished *my gun* at *him!*

Just when a sanguinary battle seemed imminent he waved his hand, and, honour being satisfied, we departed.

I took the number on his tail, by the way, and rang his squadron up that evening to tell him what I thought of him!

Feeling in rather a chastened mood, I beat it back home, and having successfully thrown the scout on the floor, reported to the squadron commander.

"Well, where did you go?"

I told him.

"Um! Get fired at?"

"Not quite, sir!"

"See anything of interest?"

I told him about the kite balloon. He nearly collapsed.

"Oh, you damned young fool, it would have served you just right if he had shot you in the—um! All right, you can go on patrol this afternoon."

I then hied me to the mess to see how the new mess waiter made cocktails.

CHAPTER 6

A Bomb Raid

After a few days' fairly uneventful line work, the flight received orders to act as escort to a bombing raid. On the night before the day on which the raid was to take place, we received operation orders which stated concisely the time of our departure, the rendezvous, and height at which we were to meet our convoy, the exact position we were to take up, the place to be bombed, and the exact route which would be pursued to and from it.

At five-thirty in the morning our six machines were all lined up ready to start. We gathered together on the grassy turf, round the flight commander, and drank mugs of hot coffee while he gave us all a few last directions, which, as none of us had ever done a bomb raid before, were very helpful.

"Above all," he said, "don't stray away from the formation. I've told you all your exact positions. If you see any of our machines straying, dive at them and shepherd them back. Don't watch the effect of the bombs, but keep a specially wide open eye for Huns, as the bombing machines will be intent on hitting the target, and coming back, keep your stations precisely and watch your tails for pursuing Huns. I shall fire a signal light when the bomb raid breaks formation and you will then join me, and we'll all come down together. It's not unlikely that some of you chaps may have a scrap with a Boche. If you do, remember that you're a dashed sight better pilot than he is, keep your head, and don't forget your gunnery! If you fire wildly about you'll probably shoot down one of the raiding machines, and we couldn't very well accept their invitation to dinner this evening!"

He glanced at his watch.

"Well, gentlemen, we meet them at nine-thousand over Bethune—Come on!"

"We completed the fastening up of our heavy leather coats and fur lined flying helmets; flying kit is very important "over there" on account of the sometimes lengthy periods spent at great heights when it is intensely cold, and a cold, numbed man cannot think and act as quickly as a warm one, and in air-fighting only instant action makes the winner. Like the others I had made my preparations thoroughly, and in a very few minutes was sitting in the machine with the engine "ticking over" ready to get away. The rest of the flight looked very picturesque as they stood lined up, their metal work and polished wings reflecting shimmering spots of crimson from the newly risen sun.

The flight commander turned in his machine and looked inquiringly down the line, and, receiving an answering wave from each be-goggled and furry pilot started off, making a wide circle for us to cut across and join him. I pushed open my throttle and in a few yards was off the ground and climbing at a very steep angle.

We all closed in on our leader, whose identity was indicated by two coloured streamers fixed to his tail. After one wide circle of the aerodrome, the flight commander headed for Bethune, climbing rapidly all the time. The morning air was very chilly and the ground partially obscured by early mists, but I felt very pleased about things in general, as the engine was going like a clock, and the machine climbing with the best of them.

I don't think I have yet described the type of scout we were flying. She was a very small machine with a short chocolate grey painted body, or fuselage, and short narrow wings. The body had a single seat or pilot's cockpit and into this I fitted pretty snugly so that just my head rose out of the opening. Just in front of my head was a curved wind screen, which was very useful considering we were doing nearly two miles a minute! My feet came very close to the engine, the top of which was hidden beneath the polished metal cowling, for streamline purposes. Between me and the engine were the machine guns.

I may mention that machine guns very often fire through the propeller field, an ingenious mechanism preventing the gun from firing for the instant the blade passes its muzzle.

To feed the guns a good big belt of ammunition was carried, and Lewis guns were used also, the ammunition being contained in round drums somewhat resembling circular dishes.

My little "office" contained me, the engine, machine and gun controls, and the instrument dashboard, in which was set the different recording dials—the engine revolution counter, height recorder, air speed indicator, etc.

Behind, the fuselage tapered down to the tail, which was comprised of the tail planes, elevators and rudder. The main planes themselves were situated in such a way as to give me a very good field of vision—an extraordinarily important point.

At first sight, the whole machine seemed so ridiculously small, with its little wings and body tacked on behind its very powerful engine, but everything about it was built for speed and quick manoeuvring, the result being that the type was a holy terror to the Huns on account of its high speed, climb, and extraordinarily rapid stunting ability.

Although all apparently exactly alike, there is always a marked difference between machines. At the front the pilot's machine naturally comes before any other consideration, for on its efficiency there depends not only his own life, but possibly matters of much greater importance.

After a while one becomes very attached to a machine, loves it almost like a living thing, and hates to see any other pilot as much as touch it!

But to return to bombing.

We found our convoy, about nine thousand feet over Bethune, climbing in great wide circles and waiting for us to join them. These were two-seater machines carrying a pilot and observer, it being the latter's duty to deal faithfully with any Huns that might appear, with the aid of his machine guns. We swung in behind them and took up our stations.

In two or three minutes, a coloured light drifted through the air from the leader and all machines closed on him and each other, thus "tightening up" the formation.

It is necessary that any machines going over the lines shall be banded together closely into these formations, so as to be able to carry our concerted attacks or defence against the enemy as the fact that they are in formation enables them to successfully vanquish what are very often most overwhelming numbers.

For instance: Three of our scouts were attacked by twelve Huns over the Ypres Salient.

The scouts formed themselves into a small circle and flew round and round watching each other's tails, in the meantime vigorously firing at the Huns, who hung about just over them. The Huns, although four to one, speedily drew off and flew back east, upon which the three scouts immediately chased them and gave them a devil of a rough time!

This shows what sheer determination can do against heavy odds.

Our entire formation now consisted of about forty machines, the bombers being grouped closely but regularly behind their leader in very much the same way as wild geese—in wedge shape—while we scouts flew over and about them on the watch. In another five minutes, everything being apparently to his satisfaction, the leader swung off and headed east, closely followed by his flock.

We were off!

The bombers were now about ten thousand five hundred feet in the air, we a little above them, and all heading straight over the Loos Salient, the lines slowly drifting towards us until I looked down to find we were directly over them.

Now the raid was met by the full attentions of the very energetic "Archie," the anti-aircraft gunner.

About the opening of the war, there was a popular music hall saying much in use—"*Archibald, certainly not!*"—in fact it became a sort of catch word. The original squadrons of the flying corps who went overseas with the "old contemptibles," being much amused at the then very mediocre efforts of the German gunners, dubbed them "Archibalds," a name which has ever since stuck, although their shooting has unhappily much improved.

The "Archie" who was now firing at us lived on a motor truck somewhere in the region of La Bassée and had the reputation of being an unpleasantly good shot. He never actually hit any of my squadron, as far as I can remember, but he certainly got infernally close to it. Neither was his lack of success due to lack of trying.

Being a little hit above and rather behind, I watched his shells burst with rather more interest than anything else.

The gunners were making a special mark of the leader and he appeared to be having a pretty warm time of it, so much so that he was forced to continually alter his course a little so as to deceive the gunners. Archie then began to deal with the main body, firing, so to speak, "into the brown" of them. All the machines, however, carried on quite uninjured, and then suddenly we got it!

Being "Archied" for the first time, or for the matter of that, at any other time, is anything but a dull experience. It rivals the side shows at a big fair for thrills. After the war a second Barnum will probably charge ten cents at some joy city for visitors to go up to be shot at, money being returned to the relatives of a direct hit!

Three or four large black balls of smoke, accompanied by a bright flash, suddenly appeared most horribly close.

The sound of the explosion is very difficult to describe. The best simile I can think of is someone bursting a huge paper bag underneath a blanket, the result being a curious coughing sort of bang!

However, *muffled* or not, I thought the war a most dangerous business to be connected with! I sheered off rapidly from the first three bursts and nearly ran into two more underneath me who gave me a terrific upward bump. This bump put the "wind up" me pretty much, for I made sure we'd been hit, and I had an instantaneous vision of a nice long drop all to myself, with a big fat bump at the bottom! After all it's the bump and not the drop which counts!

Under my Archie-inspired hand, the scout must have resembled a huge and agitated jumping bean, as fitted with hot tray! It certainly did some remarkable stunt flying, which, although I did not know it, was rapidly reducing my flight commander to hysterics, as he watched our efforts to dodge.

Having scorched about the heavens for some time and accidentally ran into nearly all the shell bursts that weren't intended for me, I calmed down, and began to feel beastly ashamed. Everyone else seemed to be flying along as though Archie was merely a rumour!

A rather curious thing happened after this. My flight commander, having been reduced by his laughter at me to an almost weak state, started to extract his little whiskey flask from his pocket. Just as he had opened the stopper, a lonely Fokker suddenly loomed up to his right front, with the laudable intention of shooting him down, whiskey and all!

Carefully recorking the flask and replacing it in his pocket, my flight commander turned calmly round and immediately shot the Hun down.

This being done to his satisfaction, he resumed his uninterrupted "Manhattan" or whatever was in the flask!

The lines were now somewhat behind us and no Archie spoilt the air and the view. The formation flew on in a steady uninterrupted course. I saw three or four Huns much lower down, but they did not attempt to come near us, which was a rather sound policy, considering they would have had about forty extremely hard nuts to crack. We scouts dodged about and around and generally played the part of watch dogs.

One of the bombing machines began to stray considerably away from the formation, and one of our scouts immediately made a furious dive at it, passing so close that it recoiled hurriedly back to the flock and remained there!

Five minutes later another bombing machine fired a signal light of a colour which meant "Engine failing," and turning round in its tracks, started to struggle back to the lines.

One of the scouts immediately went down and flew beside it, accompanying the lone and rather helpless machine back to its aerodrome, to protect it from injury, and see it, if its engine willed, into safety!

They both disappeared together, and the whole thing looked, I thought, rather fine.

I was paying a great deal of attention to my own engine and listened to it with a very anxious ear. It continued, to my great joy, to run perfectly smooth and faithfully. We were now approaching a town, and as soon as we got into range Archie began. The Germans must have had two or three batteries at this place, for the shell bursts were very thick indeed. In addition to Archie the raid was treated to another shape of Hun pleasantry in the form of what the Flying Corps had dubbed "flaming onions."

These "flaming onions" were huge rockets of balls of phosphorus which burst at the top of their climb and spread out into a great umbrella shaped curtain of flame, and sank slowly down, the idea being that any machine in its path would be instantly set fire to by the burning phosphorus.

They are very annoying contrivances, for fire in the air is a nightmare which every pilot tries not to think of, but to universal British satisfaction the flaming onions did their flaming several hundred feet below the raid.

Having passed by the town and got out of range, we saw our objective in the distance and in the course of time drew up to it.

The bombing machines now spread out a bit as each pilot devoted his attention to his bomb sights.

A bomb dropped from an aeroplane naturally makes a curved drop, as it is projected into the air from the machine at the machine's air speed, the muzzle velocity being about one hundred miles an hour, as it were. This requires the bomb to be dropped a considerable time before the machine is over the objective, and to make this process accurate a bomb sight is used and the pilot is enabled to make arrangements for wind, height, etc., but it still remains no particularly easy matter to hit a small object like a railway station from a height of ten or eleven thousand feet.

Therefore, while they were immersed in the actual progress of Hun strafing was our time to keep our especially wide open as the flight commander had told us. But no Huns interrupted our proceedings. I took one peep at the place we were bombing and saw clouds of smoke hanging over it. The leader was now flying in big zigzags so that the last machines to drop their bombs could join him.

After a short while they all straggled in and the flock gathered itself up again into a compact body, greatly to our relief, and we set off back to the lines, thirty miles away, with the comfortable feeling that we must have stirred the Huns up pretty considerably! I pictured to myself numbers of the gentle Huns below running round in little circles and cursing us for our frightfulness! The trip back was fairly uneventful until we got almost in sight of the lines, when a formation of Huns appeared flying at our own level, coming down from the north.

Without an instant's hesitation, the raid leader turned off and the whole formation headed for them, the scouts meanwhile, using their extra speed to get up in the front of the bombers.

The Huns perceptibly edged off to the east. Our raid leader edged off too.

The Huns were then smitten by the overpowering notion of beating it while the going was good, and turned back north.

One of our scouts was about three hundred feet higher than anyone else and well to the front, and he evidently thought he had a good chance to get the tailmost Hun, for he suddenly dived, with his engine on, at his quarry.

The Hun saw him coming, went into an absolutely vertical dive, and the two of them—pursuer and pursued—went hurtling down at a terrific pace, probably well over two hundred an hour, our man firing all the time.

However, as all the scouts had strict orders not to go away and leave the convoy unprotected, he pulled out after about two thousand feet of diving and climbed back up to us.

This little interlude being over we resumed our original course, everyone feeling very elated.

Despite my admitted nervousness, even I couldn't help feeling very excited and almost warlike! It struck me as being a very good show for the Flying Corps that all these machines could go calmly over thirty miles of enemy country, methodically destroy their chosen prey, and as calmly return, while all we ever saw on our side of the lines was an isolated Hun rush across at great height and bolt back again, probably to receive the Iron Cross for this death-defying deed!

The by now familiar brown scar came into sight—the trenches again. When one is on our side one looks at the line with a gloomy eye, and mutters nasty things about the war, but when one is returning from a long raid, one welcomes it with a quite affectionate feeling!

After the usual dose from Archie we crossed over. The scouts were now especially lively round the tail of the raid in case a pursuing formation of Huns tried to catch it off its guard. We saw several enemy scouts wandering about in the distance but they did not attack.

The bombing machines now throttled down, and fell away from us in their glide back to their aerodrome. I circled round the rearmost one and waved my hand at him, upon which the observer stood bolt upright on his seat and waved his goggles, with the other hand in his pocket! I was rather impressed.

We all landed together and talked over the raid for a little while; the pilot who had chased the Hun being especially pointed on the subject of Teutonic courage!

Having passed a unanimous resolution that the war, and the Flying Corps in particular, had anything else beat, we dispersed to give a look to our machines before going up to the mess.

I could not help giving mine a caressing pat on her chocolate grey cowling; after all, she'd done the job, not I, and done it so well!

I glanced up to see my next door neighbour smiling at me, as he stood leaning on his machine.

A look of great understanding passed between us.

We were learning!

Chapter 7

Scrapping

The other five machines all had their propellers gently running and were ready to start, but my mechanics were still working furiously on my engine.

The flight commander impatiently waved for me to come to his machine, and I ran over to speak to him.

"What's the matter? Why aren't you ready to start?"

"My engine is missing badly, sir, and I am changing plugs. I've just brought her down from a test and I think that's where the trouble is."

"Well, it will take you about five minutes to get them changed, won't it?"

"Yes, sir."

"Well, I'll have to start without you. Did you see the operation orders for this flight?"

"No, sir."

"We are to do an offensive patrol on the Hun side, at fifteen thousand. I'll take the formation in over the Loos Salient and will make a sweep round to Arras. It's now 3 o'clock. You be over Arras at three-thirty at about fifteen thousand and I'll pick you up. You can't fail to find us. Is that clear?"

"Yes, sir!"

"Right oh! Bye bye!" he shouted, and took off, followed by the other four. I rushed back and expedited matters as much as possible, changing the spark plugs. Directly this was finished, I jumped in and tested the engine, which happily ran perfectly, and then pushed off to keep my appointment with the flight commander.

There was an easterly wind that afternoon which was blowing up big heavy banks in places. I ran through some loose scud at about six thousand but the main body—big thick *cumulus*—was rather higher.

I kept her nose pointing towards Arras and climbed rapidly and in another minute or so spied what seemed to be an opening in the cloud bank, went up through it, and then had one of the greatest experiences of my life.

I was flying up an immense Grand Canyon of the clouds, between two gigantic cloud banks. A few hundred feet below me they joined each other, and from that swept up in the shape of a narrow V to their brilliant snowy white crests, at least three thousand feet above. All the way down the sides appeared wonderful changes of colour—deep blue caves and mysterious tunnels, great promontories jutting out like white rocks on their parent mountain. My wing tip touched one of these caps and wafted away a giant handful of soft cotton wool. I almost expected to see it hanging on the planes.

I flew on another three or four miles, the walls receding further from the wing tips as I climbed to the heights of this valley of mystery, filled with awe, and feeling so very infinitesimal amidst the snowy majesty of this untrodden, virgin world, the blue sky above, the clouds around, and the earth completely blotted from existence.

But eventually I left it behind me and the earth came into view again ten thousand feet below, a dim brownish blur in the afternoon haze, and I discerned Arras just below me. Down to the south and east there appeared thick banks of clouds, stretching as far as the eye could see. Over these clouds appeared numbers of curious little black puffs, standing out in extraordinary contrast against the dazzling cloud table—German anti-aircraft guns were firing through the gaps.

To the north the sky was clear, and it being down sun, the earth was very distinct, and I could follow the lines right up round a whitey grey flat blur—Ypres. Further north appeared a marvellous sight. For the coast line was plainly visible, against the long and seemingly narrow blue sea. Narrow—for on the horizon lay a line, as thin as a hair, of dazzling white—the cliffs of England!

It seemed to me a most extraordinary paradox; there was I sitting over the trenches, the black shell bursts from the German batteries dotting the sky, scores of machines battling for the mastery, my undercarriage wheels centred against the brown churned up trenches; here was I, in fact, right in the middle of the Great War.

Yet, just under my left wing tip, lay England!

The dashboard watch showed three-thirty, just as my flight appeared, bunched together like a small flock of geese, coming in from the east, and I dived in and took up my station while the flight commander swung back across the lines again.

We got the usual outburst from Archie, but he was not very accurate that afternoon, so we treated him with contempt.

At our high level we were above most machines, but passed by one or two of our scout formations engaged in a similar job to our own—Hun hunting.

Six hands grasped their gun controls, and six pairs of eyes eagerly scrutinised each formation as we swept up to it at over a hundred miles an hour, but up to now only the familiar red, white and blue rings met our gaze.

However, we wore now flying northeast and knew that it was most likely only a matter of time.

Suddenly a brilliant coloured light burst into flame just over the flight commander's machine—he had fired a signal!

In our code its colour meant—"Am about to attack—Close on me—"

Down went his nose as he commenced to dive followed by the rest of us. Half hidden by the leading machines, there appeared, about a thousand feet below, a formation of one—three—four—seven—yes, seven machines, and on each wing tip appeared a small, regularly formed black cross.

Our whole formation was now diving practically in a vertical line, and the screaming shrill of the air became almost unbearable. I glanced for a second at the dial of the speed indicator—one hundred and ninety miles an hour!

Our leader had dived at a point behind the Huns, and now, flattening out from the dive in a great curve, the formation dashed into the middle of them.

A fight in the air is so extraordinarily rapid that eternities seem to pass in a few seconds and no clear picture can be memorised until some time afterwards.

The flight commander was leading and was the first to engage a machine. He drove down on the enemy leader, closer and closer, until it seemed that the two machines were locked together. Then streaks of flame leapt from the muzzles of his machine guns.

The Hun pilot pulled his machine up into a great upward bound, and did a splendid turn almost upside down back to his aggressor; but the commander was too old a hand to be caught. He had followed the Hun yard by yard, and was even then circling round behind the latter's tail, firing continuously.

The Hun suddenly spun round on one wing tip, and doubling in his tracks, dashed back through the rest of his machines, but always relentlessly followed by his implacable enemy.

Then the Hun did a half loop clean over his adversary and performed a very clever turn at the top of it. It was so quick that they lost each other for a second.

A fraction of a second more and they found themselves; both machines dashed at each other and simultaneously two streaks of fire appeared from their respective gun muzzles. Still they held on until it appeared they must crash and fall in pieces together.

Then the Hun machine careened wildly up on one side and a great gout of flame burst out from its nose. It dived a few hundred feet and then wrenched back till it pointed almost straight up. It was now a mass of flames from end to end. One of the wings dropped off and fell away.

Simultaneously the machine gave a great lurch and dropped like a stone—a mass of charred wood and red hot steel, carrying its pilot down his last awful dive to death, fifteen thousand feet below.

In the meantime, the rest of the machines had been vigorously engaged and much fighting had taken place.

One of our machines fell spinning down, obviously out of control, but its passing was so quick that it was scarcely noticed.

A Hun machine suddenly left the fight and went down with its engine running "all out" in a vertical line as straight as a ruler until it crashed into the earth. The pilot must have been killed or mortally wounded and fallen forward on his controls. A few mad minutes, a futurist picture-like impression stamped on the memory, of the whirl of machines and hammer of guns—the malignant *ssip-zrrip* of enemy bullets tearing through fabric—then the show was over as suddenly as it begun. Three enemy machines diving madly away to escape, and five of ours left collecting together once more under their leader, and the flight was resumed.

The whole fight had occupied probably under three minutes!

A typical instance of modern air fighting. No more Huns were fought that trip, although several were seen, too far away to be got at, and the formation returned to its aerodrome. We got out of our machines and silently removed our flying kit, and then the flight commander, his eyes hard and his mouth set, walked past us to report to the squadron commander, that we had forever lost—— Oh, his name doesn't count. A man we all liked and respected, worthy of the great corps: And also to tell of four Huns shot down to avenge him.

As I walked down to the mess there rang in my ears the end of a little speech I had heard in England from a senior flying officer.

—and remember this! If the Flying Corps is ordered to do a job, whether you come back or whether you do not, *the Flying Corps does that job!*

CHAPTER 8

Mainly About Two-Seaters

Gales, low clouds, occasional rain, and many other atmospheric hates do not stop the Flying Corps very much, but there are times when observation is impossible.

On one Sunday we were treated to a continuous heavy rain, accompanied by fog, and flying was out of the question. Nevertheless we spent the morning on the aerodrome, in case things cleared up. However, the official weather reports prophesied a continuance of these conditions, and after lunch the flight commander and I decided to visit a certain artillery squadron some distance away, as we had a mutual pal there, and having obtained the squadron commander's permission, we set off in a car to splash our muddy way through most depressing scenery.

Heavy rain and fog above, the flat, uninteresting countryside of Northern France, and feet of mud beneath are calculated to depress most people, particularly when contrasted with pictures of a snug little house somewhere north of the Channel, with bright fire—the tinkle of teacups—and someone piloting the teapot! At such moments one is liable to detest the sights around with unusual frenzy.

At my request, we made a short detour through Bethune. This city is not so frightfully knocked about as I expected, but was certainly much dented, and the main square has been strafed quite a little.

At one time the Hun used to "crump" Bethune daily with the greatest regularity. Sometimes he would start at 8 o'clock, then he shifted to 2 o'clock, and had now adopted teatime for his attempted frightfulness. Great holes in walls, shattered roofs, and a generally moth-eaten appearance characterised that part of the city we passed through.

Having no wish to share the city's afternoon close we hurried on.

Some while after leaving Bethune we met a convoy of homely London buses, full of Tommies.

Some of the buses affected a dignified cover of grey paint, but quite a number still set forth the attractions of Mr. Pears Soap, or exhorted those suffering from *ennui* to "Go to France and Fight for your Country!"

Their destination boards still bravely announced that the 'bus was bound from "Piccadilly Circus—Hyde Park—South Kensington—Hammersmith," etc., etc. The Tommies inside were smoking furiously and vigorously singing the latest music-hall ditties with as much *joie-de-vivre* as if they were just going to get off at Piccadilly Circus!

In due course we arrived at our destination, having lost our way several times, and were eagerly welcomed by our hosts.

Their mess was in a long hut. Inside, tea was just being served, and numerous officers, with the aid of improvised aeroplane wire toasting forks, were making toast in front of the huge fire at one end.

We were immediately surrounded by a crowd of anxious querists—"Can't I lend you a dry tunic?"—"Look here, do come and change into some of my clothes!" or "Which will you have—whiskeys and sodas, or tea?" "Can we offer you a hot bath or a John Collins?" and so on, and so on.

We were led by a pack of merry khaki-clad schoolboys up to the fire and installed in the squadron's pet wicker armchairs and supplied with all we deigned to accept. Although we were perfect strangers to most of them, we might have been long lost rich uncles, or most intimate pals! No one worried over formality.

Hospitality in the Flying Corps in the field is extraordinarily keen, and squadrons like to visit each other as much as the exigencies of the service will permit. Some of the merriest hours of my life have been spent during the long winter evenings in France, as a guest or part host, while the war, and next morning's raid, was forgotten; while we talked of the latest gossip from our little village of London!

After tea we lounged and smoked and heard many a tale of the squadron's doings—but never told by the doer!

A Jones would recount the exploit of a Brown, while the latter blushed and threw cushions at him, and then the Brown would turn round and tell about the Jones, much to the latter's embarrassment. Many a tale did one hear thus, in odd snatches and laughs, which would have thrilled the quiet people at home.

Our hosts' squadron was famous throughout the Flying Corps for its stout work, and the ribbons on the tunics of those around told a tale. With their great powerful two-seater machines, they and their observers bombed the enemy, photographed him, shot him with their machine guns, controlled scores of batteries by wireless against him, and generally did him the maximum amount of harm to the square mile per minute!

Artillery ranging is a science. One might say, a science of doing a lot of things, each one important, at once, and doing them all well.

Ye gods and little fishes! In their day's work, not to speak of the night, these people crammed bucketfuls of Life—Life with a large, large L!

For instance, just to recount some episodes: The pilot, with his observer, had just furnished a somewhat tiring artillery shoot, and having watched the target slowly disappear under most excellent management, they finally finished the job. The pilot being especially "full of beans," he then headed in over the lines, seeking what he might destroy with the bombs which he had safely ensconced in their releasing racks beneath the machine. These had been given him to drop on the most suitable target which offered itself.

They both possessed, to say the least, reckless temperaments, and knew each other's capabilities to a T, which resulted in a very adventurous alliance, and that afternoon the pilot felt determined to stir the Hun trench with a very vigorous rod! He accordingly glided down to about two thousand feet and flew about some distance behind the lines, looking for some deserving receptacle, being vigorously machine-gunned at intervals. He had nearly decided on a small railway station when he noticed two trains, one in the north and one in the south, steaming towards each other on the double track.

He immediately rushed off about a mile away and watched their progress, descending still lower in the process until he was only a few hundred feet high, and then began to edge back. Both trains appeared to be going quite fast, and when they were about a quarter of a mile apart, he dashed in and arrived well between them.

By this time the trains were almost on top of each other and could not retire except by going forwards!

Flying low over one of them he waited until it was abreast of the other, and then jerked the bomb release.

By a miracle of aim he dropped his "eggs" exactly between the two trains, which were immediately blown out sideways like a pack of cards. That they were troop trains was immediately proved by the fact that grey coated Germans began to stream out of the uninjured coaches, while others struggled from the wreck. The main body, however, immediately started to bolt at the sight of the hostile machine.

Circling low down, the pilot kept the machine as steady as possible while the observer poured in drum after drum of machine gun fire, following the fleeing enemy and relentlessly mowing them down in sheaves. He was counted the best gunner in a famous squadron, and by the time he had finished his large stock of ammunition, and they were flying back home, they left but two wrecked trains and hundreds of killed and wounded Hun soldiers.

Just a ten minute job out of the day!

These machines and their owners simply didn't care a damn for anything or anybody! Four of them, one afternoon, led by a friend of mine, were attacked when over the Hun lines by twelve Hun scouts of much superior speed and manoeuvring ability. The four machines bunched closely together and resolutely faced the Hun formation, whose efforts were all directed in getting behind their tails, where they could shoot and not be shot at so effectively.

The British pilots and observers, however, were all seasoned, experienced men and there was no trick of the game that they did not know and use just a fraction of a second before the enemy.

Although they were far from home and with superior machines in superior numbers arrayed against them, the two-seaters felt very pleased with life, and "laid on" in the most approved Macduffian manner, all the time keeping the Huns in front of them and using all their gunnery wiles to bring them down.

One observer's life was poisoned for days by a dreadful stroke of fate. In the midst of the show a Hun scout appeared barely twenty feet above his gun, in momentary ignorance of what lay beneath him.

The observer, with a happy sigh, took an instant bead at the exact spot on the machine that the pilot was sitting in and pulled the trigger. The gun jammed!

He afterwards told of how that Hun stuck there for nearly five seconds while he nearly cried with mortification!

Surprising as it may sound, the twelve Huns drew off and made east, carefully observed in their retreat by the watchful two-seaters, who refused to turn tail until they were well out of striking distance. On their way home the redoubtable four were once again attacked, but this time the enemy was shot to pieces by one of our scout formations which suddenly appeared in the middle of the proceedings.

Finally, having thoroughly enjoyed themselves, they returned to their aerodrome and spent the afternoon having new wings fitted, having been, in the words of their air mechanics, "All shot to H—ll!"

A few days previously this squadron, in conjunction with another, carried out a big raid. Unfortunately one of their number had a mishap with his engine and had to return. It was speedily put right and he decided to go up again, as he calculated that he would be in time to go over and meet them before they crossed the lines again.

As a matter of fact, by the time he was crossing the lines, the raid was coming out a few miles further down; it had been a successful raid, and the Hun, stung to fury, had collected a whole crowd of machines to chase them. As the raiders were gliding back to their aerodrome their lonely compatriot was pounding blissfully along to where he thought he would meet them, instead of which he suddenly came face to face with half the German flying corps, which had been stirred up by the raid, and was immediately shot down!

Fortunately he was not killed, but, I believe, taken prisoner.

There was a certain two-seater squadron which was among the first to use a brand new type of machine. It was (and is still) a magnificent machine and very fast at an altitude.

Flying at between twenty and twenty-two thousand feet, they would select a Hun formation far below them, probably four times their number, and dive clean through them, shooting their uttermost *en route*, and then, aided by their terrific momentum and splendid climbing ability, rush back up through the petrified Huns and leave the latter two or three thousand feet below again, gnashing their teeth in futile rage, while our men rolled almost helpless in their seats with merriment!

A certain squadron very near us possessed two-seater pusher machines of great power. The pilot sat just in front of the engine, and just in front of them was the observer's cockpit—a very large roomy apartment—furnished in the most tasteful style, with Lewis guns, ammunition drums, bomb releases, and similar knickknacks.

They were a fine squadron, whose observers were especially *blasé*. No one along that front ever saw one of their observers sitting in his seat in the ordinary manner; they always passed one by sitting on the cowling and negligently kicking their heels over the edge, or else they would have climbed back and be sitting on the radiator to keep warm! Sometimes they used to change round and the observer flew the machine back. Here it may be said that the machine was most extraordinarily stable and dignified about its flying and never did anything unladylike in the air except at the vigorous manipulation of their pilots.

Amongst others, this squadron was fortunate in the possession of two very bright and comic spirits in the shape of a certain pilot and his observer, who had flown a great deal together. They scrapped like the devil on the ground and in the air, but each secretly thought the other an uncommonly fine fellow!

The pilot I will call Arty, but the observer must be left unnamed, as he is too well known to risk disclosures. Arty fixed up a thin but strong steel tube, which stuck up about three feet above the nose of the machine. At the top was a buckle which was attached to a strong little belt buckled round the observer's waist. The observer would then stand bolt upright with his feet on the narrow edging of the machine and, the rod hidden by his coat, present a most extraordinary sight. Of course, their squadron got used to them and nothing they could do surprised them.

One day, however, Arty got to hear that a certain senior officer was being taken for a joy-ride over the lines by a pilot of another squadron. He got the adjutant to 'phone up and innocently inquire what time the great man was going up and where.

Possessed of this information, Arty and his heavenly twin conspired together, went up near the lines, and then watched out for the arrival of the personage. This was easier than it sounds as they watched his machine climb up from the aerodrome.

When it was about a thousand feet below them, the observer stood up and buckled himself to the iron rod, after which Arty dived at his unsuspecting prey underneath.

The personage was then electrified by the sight of a strange machine whirling and diving and doing mad stunts all round him with its observer calmly standing on the top of it with his arms folded. When the machine did a vertical bank the observer remained in exactly the same position, jutting out sideways over a clear drop of ten thousand feet.

Having nearly induced syncope in the by now almost paralysed personage, they loosed off a round or two from the Lewis, and disappeared as suddenly as they had come, leaving the great man still clutching the sides of his machine in a petrified daze, while his pilot continued the journey.

As the two scapegraces glided down the observer unshackled himself and leaned across talking to Arty; when they were about a hundred feet from the ground, the observer got back into his cockpit and idly grasped the butt of the machine gun.

Just at that moment they had a very bad bump, and the machine dropped violently, with the result that the observer was flung clean over the side, still clutching the machine gun, and hung alone in mid-air! It was "one of those moments"! But the pilot realised what had happened in a flash, and pulling the machine violently an scooped the observer back into his seat like a pancake into the frying pan.

The observer, not unjustifiably infuriated by the whole proceeding, reached back and pummelled Arty vigorously, and tried to pull his hair out by the roots, while the miserable man cowered in his seat and tried to ward him off. All this at about fifty feet! Holding the observer off with one hand, the pilot landed the machine with the other. It then took him quite a while to explain that it wasn't a joke at all!

They were a mad pair. But several German airmen, were they now sufficiently mortal, would confess that there was method in their madness!

Recently a pilot of a two-seater machine was announced as the recipient of the greatest honour a soldier can win. Sergeant Mottershead, Royal Flying Corps, was awarded the Victoria Cross—"for the most conspicuous bravery—"

Thousands of feet above the trenches, Sergeant Mottershead's machine was set on fire by the enemy. He immediately, with marvellous coolness, headed the machine west and glided down as rapidly as possible.

The observer seized the fire extinguisher and did his utmost by spraying the pilot to save him from the awful torture of the great red flames which roared from the splintered petrol tanks and rapidly spread around the sergeant's cockpit. But his efforts could not stem the fire.

Although suffering the greatest agony and torture from the burning petrol, this gallant non-commissioned officer, with superhuman bravery and skill, chose a safe landing ground and brought his flaming mass safely to the earth behind our lines and saved the life of his observer. The machine was so injured by the flames that it collapsed, and Sergeant Mottershead could not be extracted in time to save him from death.

To qualify for that simple bronze cross, posthumously awarded, Sergeant Mottershead saved his passenger, displayed the utmost gallantry, and gave—his life.

CHAPTER 9

A Night Stunt

Allison watched the yawning batman, who had just shaken him into wakefulness, put the lighted candle on his table, and shuffle out of the room back to his interrupted slumbers. He watched him with a feeling of intense resentment, for no man enjoys being awakened in the middle of the night, even when he knows it's inevitable!

He reached out for his watch and looked at it—3:15 a. m.! Cursing the war, then the people who ran it, and, particularly, the day he had joined the Royal Flying Corps, he wriggled out of his warm "flea bag" and started to dress. The hour of three in the morning is rarely celebrated for its warmth, and this morning was no exception. He hurriedly began piling on his clothes—two suits of warm underclothes, thick riding breeches, leather waistcoat, his tunic, flying boots, and lastly, reinforced by mufflers round his neck, his immense leather flying coat.

To the uninitiated he would have presented the appearance of a somewhat overdressed golliwog rather than an airman, but, nevertheless, he was very wise. He was about to start off to bomb X——, a large military centre some twenty odd miles away on the German's side of the lines, he expected to be in the air for at least two hours, and, as there would be no Huns about to twist and wriggle in the machine to look for, he could afford to pile on clothes and insure a comfortable warmth

He finished dressing, took his electric torch blew out the candle, and tiptoed quietly out of the old *château* which the officers of the squadron slept in, and then went up to the aerodrome, running to get warm.

The landing lights, which are large petrol flares placed to illuminate the ground for pilots' use were already in position, and his machine stood outside the hangar, vast and shadowy, half visible in the diffused light from the electrics inside the shed.

His mechanic saluted as he came up. "All correct, sir, and something hot to drink I thought you'd like, sir!"

"Splendid fellow, Jones. Hot, by Jove!" He took it thankfully, and whilst drinking it, meditated upon the fact that Jones was really a priceless fellow—seemed as wide awake as if it was mid-day instead of this beastly hour.

Just as he finished, the figure of the squadron commander loomed up out of the darkness. "Morning, Allison. Ready?"

"Yes, sir. Just going to start up."

"Have you marked out your route on the map? Show me."

Allison showed him his map, with his route marked off on it. "Righto! Smith's starting ten minutes after you—— Good luck."

Allison stooped down, and with the aid of an electric torch examined the row of deadly bombs hanging safely in their rack underneath the machine, and their release controls were in perfect order. Satisfied that they were all right he climbed into the machine. His mechanic began to buckle the safety belt around him and he was soon safely strapped in. He put out his hand and switched on the tiny electric lights which were fixed to illuminate his instruments and maps, and wiped the night moisture off their glass faces.

Having tested his engine and throttled it down again, he waved his hand for "all clear."

The ground was but fitfully illuminated by the flickering flares as he "taxied" the machine out to his starting point. It was a dark night—no moon—and a trifle cloudy. Far away to the north-west in the direction in which he was going to "take off," there was a steady glow from a large steel factory, which despite the comparative nearness of the war was kept going night and day by the indomitable French.

He turned his machine round and pointed her nose toward the factory. He knew if he kept her so he would make certain of not turning round unconsciously in the dark, and slewing off his course. One last look round the interior of his machine, switching off the little lights in order to see outside the better, and he opened the engine throttle.

The machine began to rush forward, faster, still faster, her nose kept steadily pointing to the glows from the chimneys, and, with one last bound, she was off!

Allison kept climbing in a straight line for about three minutes, and then commenced a large circle, with the lights of his aerodrome as the centre.

They began to get smaller and smaller as he climbed away from them, while odd little lights here and there began to be visible, studding the black, impenetrable carpet of darkness spread underneath him. He intended climbing for about another ten minutes, and settled comfortably down in the machine. He felt distinctly anxious, and not a little nervous, for it was the first time he had done a night job at the Front, although he had flown a good deal at night in England, and he fervently hoped that his engine wouldn't let him down, particularly the wrong side of the lines. With his mechanic he had spent a considerable time looking it over early in the night, and he knew it was in splendid condition.

Presently he switched on his little lighting apparatus and peered at the altimeter. It showed him that he had reached the height he wanted to fly at, so he turned the machine's nose easterly, and carefully watched the swinging compass card until he was steadily pursuing his mapped out course. He glanced at the watch on the instrument board—3:40! In thirty minutes' time he should be dead over his objective, X———, the railway station of which he was ordered to bomb.

The steady, even note of the engine proclaimed that it was running perfectly, and Allison began to feel more confident, in spite of the long journey before him.

Night flying has a peculiarly soothing effect on a man. After the constant strain of dodging shell fire and searching anxiously for enemies in the air during the day time, the knowledge that neither can see nor hurt one is very comforting. There is no sound but the steady drone of the engine, which merges into the senses until it is almost unnoticeable; nothing but the great, black, enveloping mantle of night all around, broken below by little odd faint pin points of light, and above, by the endless, glittering array of stars. No other living thing in the air—nothing but the comradeship of vast, filmy, indistinct masses which men call clouds, half seen as the machine rushes past them. All seems to spell peace—protection—solitude—

Then the glow of lights on the dashboard reminds the pilot that it is but, after all, the cloak of war. It is only serving him as a cloak, that he may, unseen, strike death amongst his chosen prey.

A few such thoughts flitted through Allison's head as he began to fly over what is, perhaps. one of the weirdest, most awe-inspiring and wonderful sights in the world—the lines by night as seen from the air. As far as the eye can reach, north and south, stretches the long, thin, intermittent flicker, rising and falling, dying out for a moment in places, blazing up again—the bluish white light of the star shells broken by the brilliant reddish flash of high explosives—running round the great curve of the Ypres Salient, straight again, a few smaller kinks, then out again in a great sweep round Loos, straight again, fading into the distance until it disappeared in a huge, constant dull glare—the Somme artillery. His mind pictured the ceaseless seething struggle still proceeding—even at night.

Presently he began to leave it behind and drove steadily on for about ten minutes. Then he began to search about trying to pierce the blackness ahead. Somewhere not far in front must be X———. His eye suddenly caught a faint almost imperceptible gleam. Water! That must be the great reservoir X———. He looked at his map to make sure. Yes, that was it. He saw, sure enough, just beyond the gleam, a few tiny points of light which denoted the presence of the town-lights which always seem visible however stringently darkness is insisted on!

Just away to the southeast, he perceived a small steady glow, different from any of the others, in that it was travelling. A train! He watched it idly for a moment or two, then a thought struck him, and he peered to see the direction it was taking—northeast! He hurriedly examined the map It showed but one railway line in that particular tract of country, and that led straight to X———. He looked up at the glow again—

"By Gad," he cried aloud, "it must be taking up troops or munitions to X———, to be distributed along their front! If I could only get that too!"

The little glow was rapidly approaching X——— and Allison guessed it to be about a mile from the place. He instantly decided on a plan of action—if only he could bring it off—

He looked at the altimeter.

"Eight thousand," he muttered, and reached out a hand and closed the engine throttle. Down went the machine's nose, and she commenced a long even glide towards the town, sweeping down like a great purposeful bird of prey, with no sound but the hum and whistle of the wind round the wires and planes. The Huns in X——— would never hear him approach. He kept one eye on his altimeter—seven, six, five thousand, as he continued to drop. The train was almost in X——— now. Four thousand, three thousand five—then the thing he had wildly hoped for happened. As their train came in, the Germans, who had previously kept the town in pitch darkness, suddenly lit up the railway station!

Allison shouted with joy as he saw it—he was getting lower, and could distinctly see the rectangular outline of the great glass roof, lit up by the electrics underneath. Then his excitement left him, and a cold, calm fixity of purpose succeeded.

His altimeter had crept round—three thousand—two five, two—one five—one thousand feet.

"Now!" he said to himself—and swung the machine into just the position he wanted it. One last look—a tug at the bomb release, and the machine gave a great bound as the heavy bombs fell off.

He was now barely eight hundred feet from the ground, and hurriedly opened up the engine throttle. As the faithful engine began to start, there was a brilliant flash underneath him, and a terrific upward "bump" from the explosion. He gave a rapid glance down—all the electrics in the station were out, and succeeded by another kind of light—great red tongues of flame from the ruins! Then he gave up all his attention to the engine—it was going, but sputtering badly. He began feverishly to pump up the pressure in the petrol tanks, and the sputter decreased, until the engine was once more giving out its steady, powerful roar.

Two long, thin shafts of light sprang up suddenly into the air, and began to grope about.

Searchlights—trying to find him! They would be able to hear the noise of his engine now. He flew rapidly away, urging the utmost speed out of the machine, and then after a short time, began to climb again. In about ten minutes he was once more at a safe height, and he twisted round and gazed back. A faint grey light was beginning to permeate the east, but he could just see the glow of flames which denoted his successful handiwork. He turned round again and snuggled down into his coat collar, and began to feel intensely cold and rather tired. The excitement and glorious satisfaction of having successfully done his job was beginning to fade, and he found himself eagerly looking forward to getting home—a hot bath, breakfast, and then some sleep!

And, before any of them, the vision of Jones bringing him something steaming, as he taxied in! Ah!

The tops of the clouds began to show up, very faintly at first, then stronger, until the highest suddenly caught and reflected a brilliant crimson and white dazzling gleam—the first rays of the rising sun.

The earth underneath was still black and invisible, but at this great height it rapidly became lighter and lighter. Then the light spread slowly downwards, and patches of earth started to meet his eye. Imperceptibly it spread, until he could pick out a wood here, a stream there, and presently he recognised a large wood lying close to the lines. He reflected that he was dead over the lines now—yes, there, dead ahead, he could see the light from the factory chimneys near the aerodrome. He flew on for about another ten minutes, and then cut off the engine, and commenced a long straight glide—not on to a railway station this time, he reflected happily.

He descended fairly slowly and carefully towards his aerodrome—he could pick out the hangars now—lower and lower—the flares were still out, but there was ample light to land in; then finally, the last rush along close to the earth—a few small jolts, and the machine was trundling along the ground, to come to rest nearly opposite his shed. Even as he landed he had seen a figure dart into the shed and come out again holding something in its hand.

He undid the belt, stretched his cramped figure, and wriggled out of the machine.

"Jones, you really *are* a simply priceless fellow—"

And the men of the squadron, turning out sleepily, blinking in the first rays of the rising sun, to start the day's work, beheld the vision of a very tired, unkempt looking man consuming what seemed to him the most beautiful drink of his life—steaming hot cocoa—from a not over clean battered tin mug!

CHAPTER 10

Artillery Control

A thousand feet a minute!

So said the impassive little clock face of the altimeter as the great machine, its nose pointing up nearly forty degrees from the horizontal, swept upwards to its eyrie over the lines, to keep an appointment with certain long and heavy contrivances, which, tenderly handled by numerous acolytes, snuggled coyly under quantities of artfully contrived camouflage. In other words, with a siege battery.

In front, at the uphill end of the long smooth fuselage, there quivered and roared a great engine of—oh, we mustn't say—a great quantity of horses. On top of the cowling, in a direct line with the pilot's eye, were the machine gun sights; then the oval opening which was the pilot's cockpit, the interior of which was interesting. The pilot fitted snugly down into his comfortable seat. In front of him, built into their polished board, were the dials of many instruments, mostly connected with the interior arrangements of the great engine ahead. On one side was a large but narrow drum around which was coiled a quantity of wire; the drum was connected up to a sizable polished mahogany box, equipped with many shining brass knobs and quadrants.

These were the wireless antennae and transmitters

On the opposite side a little shelf supported an ebonised Morse key, wired up to the mahogany box.

Just behind the pilot, in his circular den, lurked the observer, happily cuddling the butt of a perfectly good Lewis.

After him there came only the uninteresting matter of the tail.

Ah! but there was something else in the pilot's cockpit. A map—a wonderful map, had it but known it—and on it, at a certain spot, was drawn a tiny circle in red ink.

Now they were close to the lines, and about nine thousand up, so the pilot brought the machine level. He then unreeled the drum contrivance and a long, length of copper wire streamed out below the fuselage. A slight adjustment of one of the brass knobs, and then his fingers rapidly operated the Morse key.

He was calling up the battery below, and while doing so watched a certain little piece of apparently uninhabited earth behind our lines. A minute passed by, then his keen eyes caught sight of a tiny white letter which had suddenly appeared in the brown desert below. The battery was stating that it understood him. The free hand immediately tapped out a question; a short wait. Then the little letter was replaced by another. The battery said "Yes." He turned east and crossed the lines, and with the position of the little red circle clearly in his mind, he scanned a certain area about four or five miles from the German front line, and soon found what he was looking for, a big farmhouse with one or two outbuildings surrounded by a belt of trees. Around the farmhouse were one or two light splotches—shell holes—the whole set amid a chessboard of fields. Near the farm ran a big main road.

The whole concern looked very innocent. It didn't look a bit like one of the largest ammunition stores in that part of the country. In fact, it would have hated to have anyone even hint such a thing—especially to the keen brain many thousands of feet above it, which was even then carefully eliminating, deducting, and following up all its little surroundings!

Between that farm and the road lay a field. Just an ordinary field. No one but one of the cleverest artillery pilots on the Front would have seen that there was a certain strip of that field between the farm and the road which was too much like the rest of the field to be true! And no one else would have known that it was really an ammunition wagon track which had been carefully covered up just before the dawn. However!

Our artillery maps are very wonderful things: By merely stating a number of figures and letters one can indicate very nearly which particular hencoop corner in a man's back yard one wants destroyed, and be perfectly accurate!

The pilot made a tiny dot with his pencil just on the rim of the red circle, let the pencil swing back on it, string, and then turned the machine towards the battery. Presently he was calling down again with the Morse key: A little white letter immediately answered him; then down went a little string of figures.

The little white letter was replaced by another one.

He had told the battery exactly where to fire and It had signified that it understood him and was ready. Round went the machine again, then blissfully dozing in the afternoon sun. His fingers sought the key. A moment's pause, and down went the signal.

"Fire!"

Another pause, and then a little puff appeared quite close to the farm, but not in it.

The pilot's hand was now continuously busy with the Morse key, as he sent down a string of corrections.

Then again:

"Fire!"

Once again there was a puff, but much closer. The battery was correcting its aim.

Meantime the observer was eagerly scanning the heavens for possible Huns, but only British machines met his relieved eye, so he looked over at the pilot.

The latter's head was bent down over the side, his right hand on the Morse key, and his whole being the personification of concentration.

Another string of corrections, and the little puff appeared very close indeed; yet all still looked quiet and peaceful, and the little puff might almost have been a dust storm.

Round about the machine burst crowds of big black balls of smoke—the anti-aircraft guns. But the pilot paid no attention to them except to jerk his head in annoyance when the machine passed over them and they obscured his view of the target.

Once again:

"Fire!"

The little puff appeared right in the middle of the farm.

The pilot sent down no string of corrections this time, but merely a very short alphabetical sign.

He had told the battery that it was dead on the target.

For about a minute there was a lull. Then a whole host of puffs appeared round the farm, which was soon surrounded in a cloud of smoke from the bursting shells. They seemed to appear faster and faster and thicker and thicker—the farm and the wood were being literally torn to pieces by our shell fire.

Suddenly a brilliant flash appeared in the pall of smoke, which then settled down thicker than ever over the scene.

The ammunition dump had blown up! The battery still continued to shell the farm methodically.

The next day, where there had been a farm, trees, and covered up wagon track, except for hundreds of shell craters, there was nothing, absolutely and positively nothing!

Having sent down the official form of goodbye to the battery and having been answered, the pilot set off over the lines again. Before they went home they had a little job of reconnaissance.

The next place to receive his attention was an inconspicuous but fairly large railway station about fifteen miles from the line. His fingers now busy with the pencil on a fixed tablet instead of the Morse key. In the station yard were a number of tiny objects. He carefully counted them and noted down that so many motor trucks were waiting outside the station. He then counted the number of trains in the yards, produced field glasses, and with their aid counted the trucks. A few miles away along the road to the station moved a line of specks—a transport convoy—he noted them down.

In about ten minutes he had noted down every scrap of information about the enemy's doings that would be of any use, and the next day some Sherlock Holmes with staff badges on his tunic would be able to estimate the movements of stores and men towards that part of the Front. Scores of other reports from other pilots would come before the same officer, and the staff would be able to calculate, very nearly exactly, what the enemy was doing behind the lines!

It can safely be said that what the enemy does that we don't know about isn't worth doing! They now commenced the return journey Having plenty of petrol, and their terrific speed enabling them to outdistance any Hun if the odds were too great, they pursued a series of long zigzags north and south, carefully examining every part of the country for any objects of interest.

The pilot dropped to about six thousand over a small town and noted down a few particulars of its general appearance, and then they continued their journey.

They were by now about six miles from the lines and behind a rather quiet sector, and methodically examined all the roads in sight in the hope of catching some luckless Germans unawares, but nothing met their eye.

Suddenly the observer bent quickly over and shook the pilot's shoulder. The latter twisted round like a flash, expecting Huns in the offing, but instead the observer was pointing down excitedly in a southeasterly direction.

His eyes followed the line of the observer's outstretched hand and eagerly searched the ground, but it looked perfectly ordinary and uninteresting.

He turned back to the observer and shook his head, upon which the other man bent down in his cockpit for a few seconds, and reappearing, leaned over once more to the pilot and thrust a piece of paper into his hand.

The pilot placed it in his teeth while he worried off his gauntlet and then smoothed the paper open on his knee.

"On the road just north of the big wood, beside X—— close to group of farms, moving column of troops. Can't we engage them?"

The pilot instantly looked back and sought out the locality the observer had indicated. He traced the road past the wood up to the farmhouses and watched it intently, in the meantime having turned the machine in that direction.

And then he saw.

The white ribbon of road was obscured by an indefinitely coloured blur for some length. He scrutinised the end of the blur to see if it moved. When he first spotted it, it had been close to the farmhouses and even as he watched, it crept up abreast of them. The movement was so slow as imperceptible, but nevertheless, movement it was.

The observer was right. What a chance!

He at once let down the wireless aerial again and rapidly adjusting certain knobs on the mahogany box, hurriedly tapped down his urgent message to the artillery.

He was utilising the rarely used general call to all artillery—a call which meant instant obedience to his wishes on the part of every battery near enough to gather in the faint little message of dots and dashes coming down from the blue haze of sky away over to the east.

On the ground six or seven miles away a curious thing was happening in the artillery zones.

Battery after battery ceased fire, and their smoking muzzles began to cool while an extraordinary hush settled down along the line. Battery commanders eagerly waited by their maps for the word from their wireless operators.

Somewhere deep down in well protected dugouts, a number of gentlemen, wearing the blue and white signaller's band on their arms, were bending low over their complicated contrivance of brass and ebonite, as they feverishly "tuned up" and strained to catch the faint intermittent buzz that their aerials gathered in from the ether and delivered to the ear pieces clipped on their heads.

Then they got it! Down out of space drifted the exact location of a regiment of Germans on the march.

With incredible rapidity the signallers flashed it out again to the waiting batteries while their unknown aerial correspondent repeated his message.

Although it had been so far an extraordinary brief period, the silence around the batteries was by now uncanny.

Flying pencils speedily worked out the exact line and trajectory of their owners' guns; a string of orders shouted through megaphones, followed for a moment by intense activity from the gun-layers, and then the silence was once more shattered as the lines of artillery burst into chorus.

The pilot had spent an anxious minute whilst he signalled down his call to the artillery, repeating it over and over again so that there should be no mistake. But he knew the artillery of the entire sector could not be called off all their targets to attend him in a second, in spite of their wonderful efficiency.

Long experience had told him how long he might expect to wait, and he had accordingly directed the fire to start some little way in front of the marching column, with the intention that they would arrive at that spot as the artillery opened fire.

So he waited, tensely gripping the Morse key, ready to correct their aim the instant they opened fire. The most skilful and efficient action was necessary, for immediately they were fired at they would disperse and scatter to whatever cover they could find, and his great object was to catch them in their close formation.

Then, as if turned on by some mighty hose, a great storm of shell bursts enveloped the whole of the head of the column.

The artillery had cleverly arranged their fire into a large zone around the target, and thanks to the pilot's marvellous accuracy, they got them fair and square.

His fingers were now again busy with the Morse key, for he was traversing the beaten zone right down the column. The enemy, unprepared, were, could he have seen them, in inextricable confusion. The rear of the column broke and bolted into the fields on either side to escape the awful rain of screaming shrapnel which was being so unerringly directed at them from far above.

The pilot was now completing a piece of really artistic fire control. The concentrated fire of scores of batteries was pounding down all around the road, relentlessly tearing up hedge and ditch and field and road, and all the miserable soldiers who scrambled hopelessly to cover.

He sat for a short while and watched the progress of the storm, knowing that Germans could not run away. The observer, excited beyond measure, careless of Huns, was bracing himself against the gun mounting as he peered through his field glasses at the devastation he had caused.

A few seconds passed by, and the pilot, with a few brief letters, stopped the guns and waited for the smoke to clear away to give him a dear view of his handiwork.

When it did there was no longer a road, but a mass of shell holes. Of the regiment that five minutes before had been marching unsuspectingly along it, probably to take their places in the trenches that night, nothing was to be seen. All looked deadly still and quiet, while down wind there drifted a great cloud of dull heavy smoke.

The lives of probably scores and scores of British Tommies had been saved, and an entire Boche regiment wiped out, by just two men and a Morse key.

The pilot throttled down the great engine with the intention of gliding down low so as to observe the artillery effect there—when there broke on his ears a noise exactly resembling that created by an exasperated maid when she raps on the door to wake one up, the morning after the night before. A sound which, even in the above circumstances, is unpleasant, but doubly so when one happens to be sitting in an aeroplane, and the creator of it a hostile machine gun.

The pilot grasped the situation, if anything, a shade before the observer, and then they both acted together, in a manner which was nothing short of amazing.

The engine was again in full blast and both men extremely on the alert, as well they might be, for they had committed an unforgivable sin—being caught unawares.

For a fraction of a second the Hun, although heard, could not be seen, and then he came into view close underneath and behind their tail, carefully keeping the latter interposed between their rear machine gun and himself, while he poured in bullets from both his machine guns.

The pilot and observer were having a pretty lively time as bullets tore through the woodwork and fabric around them, but the former quickly hurled the machine over nearly on its back as he performed an acrobatic which he kept in stock for any eventuality of this description.

The Hun—a powerful two-seater—although no fool, was not able to follow them, and was momentarily at a disadvantage—a disadvantage which the British gunner made use of like lightning. The enemy machine was now below and to one side and with guns blinded by his own wings; and while the pilot held the machine in the best position for him, his Lewis gun stuttered its way through an entire drum, with the gunner's eye glued behind the sights.

By the time he was half way through it, both machines were twisting and turning round one another in a way that made shooting very difficult.

Suddenly, from the other side of them, a fresh blow was dealt, for two more Huns had appeared from nowhere, and were pouring on a veritable hail.

The observer whipped the empty drum from the Lewis and flung it overboard—there was no time to replace it in its rack—and seized a fresh one, but even as he lifted it out over the gun it was blown clear out of his hand, and half his fingers torn away by a shrieking stream of lead, while blood began to spout out from the hideous wound.

Nothing daunted, in spite of the agonising pain, he reached down and with the other hand picked out another drum, only to collapse back into his cock-pit in a dead faint.

By this time the pilot had realised that his gunner was out of action. Matters were becoming desperate. The observer done for and three Huns sitting behind his tail where he could not get at them with his gun, which only fired forward through his propeller. But he was an old hand, and had yet a good few tricks to fall back on. The unequal battle had now resolved itself into a test of flying—sheer, downright trick flying.

The great fighter spun this way and that and dived down and sprang up again under the sure, steady hand of its master whose brain, cool and resourceful, calculated every move and subtlety of his lightning game of chess he knew so well: a false move, a second's hesitation, and there was but one ending.

Against him were arrayed six determined brains, six skilful pairs of hands, as each Boche pilot and observer did his utmost to shoot, to hit, to kill.

Then with a sudden wrench and twist he had the machine round before they could follow him and dashed back through them, so close that his undercarriage almost touched an enemy; another terrific turn and he had got what he wanted—a Hun in front of him!

Crouching in his seat, his thumbs resting on his gun control fixed to the control sticky implacable—oblivions to all save one great object—to get the Hun he was following dead in front of his gun sights.

The enemy pilot realised the danger, and quickly brought his machine into the best position for his observer to fire.

The two machines were now close together, and as the British pilot glared along his gun sights, into which he had at last got his enemy, he found himself looking straight down the barrel of the German observer's gun, while its screaming thud and stutter of bullets deafened him.

He closed in nearer and nearer; the gyrating machine quieted, the gun sight steadied on the mark, and he pressed the gun release dead home.

Now the hammer of his own gun drowned everything else; an excruciating crash in his leg he scarcely noticed, but only that the hammering continued until the enemy machine, its pilot riddled reeled down out of action.

One!

His left leg had been shattered. He did not know this, but only that he couldn't operate that side of the rudder bar with it, but he still made shift with his right foot, by crossing it alternately from side to side of the rudder bar, although nearly all his manoeuvring ability was done for.

The remaining two Huns were closing in on his tail, and holding their fire until they had a certainty. Even with his high speed, they were too close for him to escape by ordinary means.

There was one move left—a risky move, but—that or checkmate. He waited for the Huns to open fire. Another second and both recommenced on him.

Throwing the machine up on its tail, he gave a wonderful imitation of being "down and out." He let her drop aimlessly over, out of control, and then, with a touch of rudder at precisely the right moment, he had her pointing vertically to the ground in a violent spinning nose dive.

The floor reeled and spun under him and the scream and shrill of the outraged wires told their own tale. The little hand of the air speed indicator was past two hundred and twenty.

If the machine had been too badly shot about—if a spar had too many holes in it—it meant death. Still he continued his mad whirling dive to earth. He held on until the height recorder had swung; round to a thousand feet, when his still cool and steady hands pulled her out level again, barely five hundred feet from the ground.

He was by now in great pain and feeling very weak, and set off westward to make the lines as soon as he could. The Huns had given him up, for the sight of that wild dive had convinced them that they had shot him down, which was just what he wanted.

The riskiest move had, after all, won.

The great machine seemed, after all their adventures, still intact, for they were now doing a level two miles a minute for home. The pain from his leg was nearly unbearable, and a terrible nauseating stupor began to overcome him.

He found himself wondering dimly whether he could keep conscious long enough to land the machine, and whether the observer was dead or only unconscious.

He leaned back in his seat, his eyes half closed, and strove to hold what little grip he still had of life—it would keep slipping—slipping—and his control of the machine was purely the last remnant of an acquired instinct.

Faintly, the sound of a machine gun chattered up underneath him, and he was dimly aware that he must be over the lines, and the Huns were firing at him.

For all his will his head began to sag forwards, and as if in a dream he saw the whole floor of the machine stained in blood. His head sagged still further. He wondered numbly about the observer.

The thought shocked the poor dazed brain like icy water.

The observer!

With an almost incalculable effort of will he raised his arm, inch by inch, up to the ignition switch, and rested his hand on it.

Then he moved his head slowly, with immense effort, and rested it on the side of the machine so that he could see over.

Very, very slowly from the back of his brain, as if through a hundred padded doors, came the faint insistence that he must get the observer down.

He dreamily watched the ground rushing past the machine: a large field appeared in front.

With a last concentrated effort his fingers closed round the switch and turned it.

The machine's nose at once sank towards the ground; the field came closer and closer; in a stupefied way he knew that they were nearly into it.

He made a terrific effort to pull back the stick and land the machine, but his arm would not move.

Then to his weary brain there descended in one blow the whole elements of the cosmos; light, darkness, earth and sky drove home a mammoth steel battering ram amid an immensity of blackness, in one crushing, terrific crash.

And yet all I could get out of them as they lay side by side, three weeks later, in the little field hospital, blinking owlishly at me through yards of bandages, was: "Oh, yes, we did a shoot, and some recco—Copped some Huns in the neck, too! Then we had a tune-up with three Boches—Old Guns there got pipped like an idiot. I toddled home with the old hen, y'know, but—I don't know, I went to sleep or something, like a damned fool, just as she was landing, so she washed, and, of course, here we are. But, look here, that infernal doctor won't let me have a smoke, so for Heaven's sake let me puff that one of yours—"

So I had to wring it out of them, bit by bit, bribing them with puffs from a cigarette, and make the rest up with a little logic.

Anyhow, they had to admit, when they read my account—"Oh, I suppose it's pretty true. But it's awful damn rot, y' know."

Chapter 11

The Day's Work

We had now been at the Front quite a considerable number of years. Or rather we considered we had. However, in prosaic everyday language, it was roughly four months since we had landed at Rouen; the four months had been lengthened into years by the extraordinary and persistent monotony of war as the Flying Corps makes it. Every day from dawn till dusk the squadron flew and was connected with some unpleasantness or other, either in aiding or abetting other squadrons in the perpetration of their various nefarious occupations, such as bombing, photography, reconnaissance, artillery, observation, etc.—that is to say, we escorted them while they worked their will on the enemy—or we committed some rightfulness of our own, mainly connected with energetically chasing the wily Hun about the Empyrean and occasionally leading him gently or otherwise to *terra firma*, which he struck with varying degrees of violence.

Every day there was the same old cold morning, the same Archie, the same breed of Hun, the same jam in the machine gun—in fact, the same everything, until, if you were darned lucky, you ate the same dinner, and dreamed the same dreams about leave after it!

No one except the pay clerk knew the date or day of the week. Sometimes we would notice a number of people standing in the road beside the aerodrome, clad in the usual black, carrying the usual infants, and we would realise that it was Sunday afternoon, and that the local inhabitants had come to pay us a visit. Beyond this, however, our conceptions of time were rather vague.

The summer had left us, and from dozing in deckchairs in the sun during the intervals between jobs of work, we now shivered, clad in our furriest coats, around small and somewhat ineffective fires.

In the air the cold had become more than a joke, and necessitated the use, by smearing, of a nauseating substance resembling decayed and somewhat thin axle grease, which the gullible believed to be "oil, whale, refined, pilot for the use of, gallons, Umph," as the enthusiastic equipment officer, a non-user, described it. This preparation was popularly supposed to prevent frostbite and it was difficult to imagine anything less than an alligator biting through its sticky crust with any success! But we were glad of it, for it is hard to conceive the intensity of the cold at a great height unless it is experienced. At twenty thousand feet on a winter's day, even the most momentary exposure of bare flesh results in very severe frostbite, while a serious problem is presented by the oil in the guns freezing and perhaps rendering the latter so stiff as to cause a complete stoppage.

Of the original pilots that had come over with the squadron, quite a number were missing, some east of the lines, some at home wounded, some transferred, some promoted, and so on. The gaps had been filled by various youthful strafers who in their turn became veterans and towered above later comers in a manner wonderful to behold.

The remainder of original personnel had become deep in cunning and guile, and Hun lore. They knew a great deal about a great number of curious things—of Huns and guns and undercarriages, of barrages and fins—so to speak. They were all a trifle morose with reference to the war and their own little bit in particular. Flying no longer appealed to them as an after-luncheon sport; instead it had become a cold and most exact science—a matter of gunnery and bluff. One or two pilots, having achieved several Hun scalps, were inclined to be bloodthirsty, but all were bored, the old hands very much and the newer ones somewhat

After all, from no matter what viewpoint the war is surveyed, even if it be from the Holy of Holies of the scouts—twenty thousand feet—it eventually cloys and loses the pristine charm it once held!

Our *ennui* was occasionally relieved by new gadgets—"gadget" is Flying Corps slang for invention! Some gadgets were good, some comic and some extraordinary.

When winter first started, some beneficent genius at home was struck with the splendid idea, that of an electrically warmed flying suit. Presumably the genius was misinformed of the severity of the cold at a great height, for he produced the most powerful system of central heating that the Flying Corps had yet experienced! The test suit was tried out by an observer in an artillery squadron close to us.

For the first few thousand feet the suit was just comfortably warm, but after that it began to develop heat at an appalling rate and in rather embarrassing places, with the result that the observer was rapidly reduced to most profuse perspiration. He had been standing up in his cockpit during the climb, and when it got so hot he sank back on to his seat somewhat exhausted. It was most unfortunate for him that the designer had placed the most powerful electrode, or whatever it is called, in such a position that the observer sat on it. As his riding breeches were a trifle thin the observer received a most painful and lasting impression of the electrode. Springing upright again the unfortunate man wildly tried to remove the garment, which fitted on as a one-piece combination suit, but owing to the somewhat cramped accommodation of an observer's cockpit, failed dismally. When he got back to earth he complained bitterly that he "was in the Flying Corps to observe, not to be branded like a blasted Texan cow!"

The more cunning of us had successfully wangled a ten-days' leave, which was of course a most exciting thing, for even the homeward journey was not devoid of interest in the least. One would start by entering a train at some unearthly hour in the morning, and at about tea time the same day the train had probably progressed quite five miles, but unfortunately nearer to the lines! Throughout the night it would rumble and clatter and crash its awesome way through northern France, and one would wake up to find one's self back near the aerodrome again.

After a day or two's chess, the train would labour painfully to the coast, and one would commence to make frantic endeavours to get aboard some sort of vessel bound for Blighty. This was generally accomplished, and after about a week's strenuous endeavour one would walk into Cox's Bank, ascertain one's balance, draw it, and become swallowed up in the haze of ten days' undiluted joy! The time and inconvenience of the whole journey is always especially irritating to a Flying Corps officer, who knows he could do the whole journey in under two hours with his machine!

Returning from leave one very often "ferries over" a new machine from an aircraft depot in England to the aircraft depot in France, a method of returning infinitely preferable to earthly and marine means on account of time alone. Therefore the end of his leave often finds a pilot with ten days of lurid life behind him, a heavy overdraft at his bank, the tears of many damsels staining his tunic, his coat collar not yet entirely free from traces of some charmingly bepowdered and delicate arm, glumly surveying a large machine, obviously new, entirely unknown to him, of unknown power, speedy and reliability and possessed of only one feature which he can recognise—a notice scrawled on the side—"F. P. W. O."—weird hieroglyphics which mean that the machine is "Full, Petrol, Water and Oil."

The officer in charge of such matters then appears and lures the saddened merrymaker into his little office, where by threats and pleading he induces him to sign numbers of army forms.

Occasionally there is an altercation.

"But look here, I am a scout pilot and don't pretend to be able to fly aerial tanks like this I I'm not going to try and waft this blooming elephant across the water. I might lose myself in it, and not be able to find the controls again. Take the filthy thing away and bury it, and gimme a scout."

Or:

"I'm awfully sorry that I can't fly scouts—I'm a two-seater pilot, and I don't think that I'd deliver this scout in France in such a way that they'd recognise it—" And many, many other wails, the complainants sometimes being inclined to pugnacity, sometimes defiant, sometimes passive resistance, while others implore. To all of them the officer in charge makes much about the same reply:

"Oh, my dear old thing, but she's simply a duck to fly—the very nicest thing the factory has produced for years I Don't you be nervous, old bean, but run along now and take her off. You'll have a most enjoyable trip, and I wish I had the chance of coming with you. Just sign this—and this—and this—Ah, that's all right! Now give my love to little Alice when you get over there. Hope you'll enjoy yourself!" And marched away, whistling blithely, bearing various documents with signatures which leave the miserable signee the total but unwilling owner of a large and powerful war machine, breed unknown, value umpteen years' pay, which a trusting government expects him to deliver intact to the British Expeditionary Force.

If he is a man of great courage he gloomily decides that he may as well be killed this way as any other, and makes an examination of the machine to make sure that it is all there. He then delves into its "office" and endeavours to master sufficient of the gadgets to render flight possible. This done, he looks round for someone to help him get away, naturally expecting assistance in some shape or other, but he appears to be the only one who expects it. In short, the mechanics, equipment officers, stray dogs, and other peculiar denizens of the great depot seem supremely indifferent to his very existence. After a time he will probably make a sortie into one of the hangars in search of help. A callow youth, rather limp about the lips, with a cigarette behind his ear, stops in answer to the questions:

"Can you start up my machine? It's an X.Y.Z. 10 A."

The youth eyes him with mild surprise, and replies in broad accents.

"Aw, noa, surr! I be a latrine guard, surr! But heer's ther c'pril over here, surr."

The corporal eyes the pilot somewhat distantly in answer to his enquiry. He looks as though he thought the pilot a poor sort of officer anyway. He evidently considers his taste in tunics rather bad, or the cut of his leather coat a trifle out of fashion.

"We—ell, I'm rather busy, sir."

Here the pilot either goes mad and is carried away frothing, or else he tries a little frightfulness.

"Why the Hades don't you stand at attention when you are talking to an officer? Take that damn cigarette out of your mouth at once. Now get an assistant and come over to my machine, and damn well hurry up, too. Don't stand there gaping like an idiot, but try and look as though you knew something or else you will find yourself in the guard room before you wake up," etc., etc.! Eventually, after several very dispassionate individuals have poked it and pulled it and generally tickled up its innermost entrails, the engine starts and violently agitates an odd dozen or so of the instrument board dials. The pilot, after a vain effort to master whether:

(a) Revolutions per minute were correct
(b) The oil pressure up
(c) The water circulating
(d) The tank pressure correct
(e) The auxiliary tank pressure correct
(f) Engine temperature just right
(g) The ignition correct at full power
(h) The cat put out
(i) The alarm clock set

and a few other trifles, dismisses the acolytes, who promptly walk off obviously indifferent to the entire proceedings. After a somewhat hectic five minutes getting used to the machine the pilot generally heads off for France, and unless he is brought down by our well meaning but energetic coast anti-aircraft batteries, successfully crosses the Channel—a matter of ten minutes—and with any luck gets the machine down safely at the depot, and from there makes his way by train or aircraft back to his squadron.

Of course, there are people who do this sort of thing continuously, and they are known as "ferry pilots"—usually men who have had long spells at the Front, have been wounded or for some cause or other need a rest but are fit for quiet flying. These ferry pilots are always most magnificently *blasé*; they regard aeroplanes with much about the same feeling with which a civilian eyes a wheelbarrow, and the Channel is to them a mere puddle. They fly a machine over to the middle of France, take tea, fly an old one back again and drift nonchalantly into dinner as coolly as if they had merely played a round of golf.

The people at our aircraft depots in France know them well. A ferry pilot will appear suddenly out of the sky, throw the machine on the ground—he sometimes really doesn't mind so very much whether it is a good landing or not, just so long as it is a landing—and step out leaving the machine like a forlorn taxicab waiting for a fare.

There follows a short and brisk interview with the adjutant—

Here's an A. X Z. 760. Here are the log books. Sign please. Any old machines going back, please? No? Well, when is the next train for the coast? Am I in time for the 4:45? Splendid! Bye-bye—see you again tomorrow.

And off he'll go and be back again in England at midnight! It can't be all beer and skittles to be a ferry pilot!

And so finally, with nerves rather shattered, one finds one's self back into the comparative peace of one's squadron at the Front. It takes quite a few bracing days over the lines to restore one's health to its pre-leave standard of efficiency, and then one settles down to another lengthy spasm of war.

During the long days of summer and then the shortening ones of early autumn and winter the squadron, in common with the rest of the Flying Corps, had been worked hard and continuously. As mentioned before, our work consisted not only of offensive patrols, or fighting pure and simple, but a great quantity of escorting, for just as the infantry is engaged winter and summer in a constant war of attrition, defence and preparation so is the Royal Flying Corps busy with its large diversity of duties.

The artillery alone, with its peculiarly intensive and sometimes microscopically accurate work, its enormous numbers—numbers vastly different from 1914—demands a great amount of the corps' attention, for the guns have become such a supremely necessary and effective part of the service for defensive as much as offensive that every effort has to be made to afford them accurate observation and control. The artillery's work is continuous, for not only is there the question of retaliation on enemy trenches, as an inducement to the Boche to cease worrying our men when they commence frightfulness on the British trenches, the destruction of numerous works in and around the enemy's trench line and sometimes far behind, but also the continuous process of registration.

Now, when a battery for some reason or other wishes to know the exact range of a certain object, let us say a farmhouse, cross roads, a wood, or any place against which it is possible it may have to fire, it first of all tries for what is called registration. A machine from an artillery squadron will accordingly effect wireless communication with the battery—the arrangements between the battery and the squadron being made previous to the machine's ascent—and proceed to "engage" the target. The battery will fire a single shell at the target, aiming as accurately as possible with the aid of the artillery maps; the machine will then correct the battery fire by wireless, and after a few more shells, each corrected and directed by the aeroplane, the battery will make a direct hit, of which fact it is informed, of course, by the aeroplane. Once a direct hit is obtained the battery carefully notes the exact elevation and line, etc. of its guns. The machine and battery will then, acting upon a prearranged plan, register onto another target, or perhaps five or six during the afternoon, according to the circumstances.

The result is that if at any future time the place registered becomes sufficiently important to war rant its destruction, the battery has merely to refer to its books and methodically destroy its target with absolute accuracy without the further assistance of aircraft. For instance—a farmhouse situated way back behind the lines, although known to be unoccupied, will be registered by the artillery. Supposing that some considerable time afterwards it comes to the knowledge of the staff that the farm has since been occupied, or is being fitted up as an ammunition dump. No action will be taken for a short time, so that the Boche may be lulled into a feeling of security and pack up his farmhouse with men or shells, or more delightful still, make it the headquarters of a general.

When our people think that the Boche has settled down to enjoy life, and probably fitted up any number of telephones, sleeping quarters, etc., the artillery will quietly step in with a brisk half hour's frightfulness and blow the whole place to blazes!

Then there are the shoots which are carried through to the bitter end—the complete destruction of the target. The target may be anything from a trench to a commodious *château*, but in any case, thanks to the accuracy of the gunners and the skilful aircraft control afforded them the result is always the same—the complete dispersal—sometimes literally—of the wily Hun and his works.

Then again there is counter battery work. This entertaining sport consists of the determined endeavour on the part of a British battery to blow a German battery off the face of the earth, and it is in order to evade unpleasantness of this description that the much talked of camouflage is used, for batteries on both sides employ numerous means, generally most painstaking and artful, to disguise themselves as ploughed fields, young trees, dead dogs, or whatever else pleases their fancy, and generally become the most retiring and hermit-like members of their respective armies. The Huns have even gone to the length of constructing dummy batteries and exploding small charges near the dummy muzzles to delude hostile aircraft into the belief that they were the genuine article, and undoubtedly they sometimes succeeded admirably until our pilots "got wise."

The point which used to arise in our minds was what unfortunate Hun was detailed to stay behind and loose off the puffs, while the supposed battery was being vigorously shelled. We could only suppose that the Hun utilises this pleasant little job as a punishment to refractory members of his rank and file!

But camouflage or no camouflage, German batteries are destroyed almost daily, sometimes hourly, while our own, thanks to the fact that the Hun stays his own side of the lines (a fact due to circumstances altogether outside his control) sit in comparative—I say comparative—safety. The casualties amongst the gallant gunners, who at all times, in common with the rest of the army, see that their job is done, and done infernally well, no matter how heavy a fire is directed against them—proclaim that this safety is after all comparative. But there is this consolation—that the German batteries are a long, long—in fact, a very long way—worse off.

If there should happen to be a push the artillery business becomes extraordinarily flourishing; but more of this in another place.

The control of artillery, without which in many cases the gunners would be absolutely blind, is not obtained without a cost. No one realises better than the enemy the vital importance of accurate artillery control, and he therefore makes every endeavour to destroy machines engaged in this work, and it becomes necessary for the artillery squadrons to be well protected by scouts, and also to be themselves of a design which renders them formidable in air fighting. Against our scouts are opposed large numbers of Hun scouts, and thus over this phase of work alone a great deal of scrapping is involved.

Then there is photography. On every day during which weather conditions render visibility decent, scores of our photography machines cross the lines and systematically carry out such work as is desired by the staff. Especially when a "Push" is contemplated is this work rendered exceptionally heavy. But quite apart from pushes, the staff is continually crying for photographic information, and when the corps is asked for such information it sees to it that it is supplied forthwith. Our cameras represent the finest instruments in the world, and the officers who use them skilful to a degree which ends in peculiarly distressing results to the gentle Boche, who considers photography, after all, a particularly ungentlemanly practice—in fact, only worthy of the dastard British! But neither his Archie, his scouts nor his huge formations have ever yet succeeded in preventing any of his strongholds from being photographed, not only once but sometimes daily for weeks and weeks, as the progress of some new work is followed.

An air photograph, to the uninitiated, represents a mere blotch of dented mud; when shown one the layman is probably politely incredulous of any serious good being obtained from it, and it is therefore an education to see an experienced photographic officer analyse the picture. Experience, education, and a keen knowledge of local circumstances make the analysis so thorough that in due course the General Staff is informed of precisely what the enemy has done, is doing, and what he probably will do. The photograph itself may have been taken at ten thousand feet or five hundred, above the trenches or forty miles behind them; it may have occasioned the loss or disablement of one or perhaps two machines and their crews; it may have taken days of endeavour against hostile forces and bad weather; but eventually, in the shortest possible time, no matter what the trouble or the cost, it is laid on the desk of the staff officer concerned and gives up to him all its secrets.

Here again the enemy naturally makes every effort to prevent the machines from returning with their photographs which once more necessitates an escort and a large amount of fighting.

After photography there comes reconnaissance—work which requires very highly trained personnel. A reconnaissance may be short—just round and about behind the lines—or long, in the shape of a forty or fifty mile trip into enemy country. By means of reconnoitring, the enemy is watched so constantly and effectively that nothing escapes our notice unless it is done under the cover of night. The ultimate result of this constant watch is that the enemy has to be extraordinarily cautious of his movements by day far back behind the lines, and to refrain from any at all within five or ten miles from the trenches. The passage of our aircraft over enemy territory is so constant that the movement of a body of troops or stores presents a very embarrassing problem, inasmuch as a column of troops or motor tracks is liable to have long range artillery fire directed at it by a reconnoitring machine, which will utilise a certain urgent artillery call by wireless and thus turn on to the target every available battery in range.

As the fire is controlled by the aeroplane, it becomes impossible to escape its efforts unless excellent cover can be got at quickly, which, even though it is available, is not always made use of, due to a temporary failure on discipline and organisation which is after all very understandable when one recollects that a battalion or so of troops may be marching happily along a road miles behind the lines, without the faintest idea that they have even been observed, and then suddenly have a perfectly fiendish deluge of high explosive shells and shrapnel showered upon them, killing and wounding perhaps hundreds during the first ten seconds.

Dismounted troops attacked in this manner will naturally scuttle at their utmost speed to decent cover, if there is any, or if they are in a bare piece of country disperse and spread themselves out under hedgerows, in ditches and generally as best they can. Unless their cover is very good, however, the rain of shrapnel will eventually find them out, and many and many a German regiment has paid the uttermost penalty for being caught in the open by one of our machines.

In case of motor trucks their destruction is likely to be singularly complete, for as they cannot take cover their only hope lies in speeding up to the best of their ability. This may succeed admirably until the first truck or two is hit, which brings the rest of the convoy to a standstill; then, unless the controlling aeroplane is shot down, nothing can save those trucks from being methodically blown off the road, one by one, and reduced to match wood.

The movement of trains behind the enemy's front is naturally an object of great interest to us and therefore his stations and railway systems generally receive daily inspection from the Flying Corps, while every detail ad to the number of trains, trucks, engines, passenger or freight cars, direction and speed of trains will be carefully noted and reported to the staff the instant the machine returns. The progress of a single train may be noted by several of our machines; for instance, a train may be observed by aeroplane A steaming northwards near Valenciennes, aeroplane B will see the same train near Condé, aeroplane C will pick it up steaming by Hollain, while aeroplane D will note it finally at rest at the station in Tournai. The reports of all these machines, coming through to the staff from the different squadrons, will be added together, and the whole progress of the train, its destination and its probable cargo become an open book to the General Staff.

Even night cannot entirely cloak the enemy's train movements; for on Tuesday evening, let us say, the staff will receive reports that fifty passenger coaches and ninety freight cars with four engines are lying in the Douai station yards. Wednesday early the first report will come in, perhaps with a photograph attached, stating that there are now one hundred passenger coaches and only twenty freight cars. The staff can thus estimate what troops or munitions went into Douai during the night. All this information, backed up as it is by scores of photographs and written reports from a great number of machines, gives the General Staff sufficient data to accurately estimate troop and store movements everywhere over the lines, which information may be of priceless value and enable any enterprise of the enemy's to be forestalled and frustrated in a manner which would be absolutely impossible without aircraft.

The ability to make fairly accurate and dependable reports of what is to be seen on the ground is naturally one which takes considerable training and experience to acquire, for an aircraft reconnaissance report is worse than useless unless it is absolutely accurate, and taking in consideration the fact that a machine may have half a dozen fights during one flight, and have to keep a constant watch in the air as well as on the ground, long reconnaissance is rendered anything but a peaceful occupation.

As regards hostile batteries, everyone, including the scouts, keeps a keen and constant lookout for gun flashes, inasmuch as a scout, although not engaged in artillery duties, may observe an enemy gun flash and report it to the proper quarters when he gets back. This will result in the noted locality being closely but unostentatiously watched by an artillery machine, which having several batteries at its beck and call, will deal summarily and with great violence with the Hun battery so unfortunate as to disclose its whereabouts.

A great deal is heard, in the press particularly, of the German raids on England, and perhaps even more from the "Man in the Street" who is generally particularly free with his criticism on the subject of retaliation.

Looking at the situation from the point of view of the absolute layman, he naturally thinks that if the Germans come over and drop bombs on non-combatants, hospitals, and anything he thinks he can hit, that the obvious thing to do is to collect hordes of aircraft and dash over far into Germany and bomb and bomb to our hearts' content, and so pay the Hun back in his own coin, and give him a worse time than he gives us.

Now let us examine this question, not from the layman's point of view but from the military side. The enemy has constructed, maintained and increased a large fleet of Zeppelins and a good many squadrons of large weight-carrying aeroplanes for the sole purpose of bombing England; the former coming over as they do under cover of night, proceed to drop large quantities of bombs upon the best target they can find, displaying an absolute unconcern as to what the target is, providing that it is inhabited. The location of targets of military value has never worried him one iota, and his great object has been the bombardment of a large city, preferably London, in which object he has occasionally succeeded, although at a heavy cost in Zeppelins and the highly trained valuable crews. Latterly he has utilised large Gotha aeroplanes to bomb London and the southeast coast with once again an absolute disregard for the nature of the target.

Margate, Kingsgate and Ramsgate have been bombed continuously, not only by the large squadrons which the enemy organises and sends over to do the job on a large scale, but by small quantities of machines which dash over from the Belgian coast, drop their bombs, and dash back again. In describing these raids Berlin has stated time after time that "our aircraft successfully bombed the fortified places of Margate," etc., the "fortified places" being popular seaside resorts possessing no single feature which even the most imaginative could describe as a fortified position. These aircraft coming over in the broad light of day can pick out their target with absolute accuracy and therefore there is no excuse for this promiscuous bombardment of the non-combatant civil population in open towns.

London itself has sustained a certain amount of material damage and loss of life which in respect to the gigantic scale of destruction of the war in general, is absolutely infinitesimal and quite apart from any ethical standpoint, insufficient to justify the expenditure of time, labour and lives on the part of the perpetrators.

Full many a time the Germans have had the pleasure of contemplating, as a result of the extraordinary bravery, dash and intrepidity of her marvellous and wonderful pilots, the magnificent damage wrought amongst us in the shape of old men, women, wounded in hospitals, and in, alas, so many cases, children, blasted into eternity by a means which they had absolutely no defence against.

London, despite the scores of raids directed against it, has not diminished its efficiency as part of the great war machine one iota, neither has any other city or town in Britain. Judging by all reasonable and decent standards there can be absolutely no justification whatever for this shedding of innocent blood, but quite apart from such standards there is nothing else by which it can be justified. As an extreme military measure the Germans might perhaps feel that the end had justified the means if their air raids had so disorganised England as to seriously hinder our armies in the field, or to have caused the population to rise and demand an immediate peace on any terms, either eventuality of which would have saved the lives of thousands of her soldiers. But this is what makes it the crime it is.

It has not succeeded!

The Germans pursued a policy of frightfulness against Belgium, the proven details of which are so revolting as to madden any decent minded human being who reads of them or sees them, for the sole purpose of wiping the country off the map.

But they have not succeeded.

They have concocted and used poison gas, and caused the most fiendish suffering and agony amongst thousands of soldiers; they have used liquid flame, the main result of which has been to burn numbers of wounded men, unable to crawl away from it, to death in a most excruciating way; they have committed wholesale slaughter of innocent women and children, such as the *Lusitania*; all in an endeavour to smash their enemies.

And in it all they never have, and never will, succeed.

If they had succeeded—if poison gas had broken the line, and accomplished our lasting and crushing defeat, they would have saved sufficient lives in their own nation by an immediate shortening or ending the war, to have rendered such means, vile as it was, justifiable in their Nietzschian eyes. If *Lusitania* crimes had so crippled our navy and merchant marine as to starve our civil population, or allow of the passage of food or munition to their own sorely tried country, they might have said it was justifiable.

But no! The Prussians have degraded themselves to a standard where hatred, loathing and contempt are the only feelings entertained of them by any normal human being who has seen their work. All the agony and misery of Belgium has resulted in nothing. In short, their enemies have so utterly disgusted the Allies that the latter are, thank God, absolutely steeled to end their besmirched and degraded military career forever.

But all this beside my point, which is that hostile air raids so far from terrorising the British public, have merely aroused their tempers and increased their determination, which facts were so very clearly shown by the huge increases in voluntary recruiting which followed the said air raids.

And now let us examine the other side of the picture—the bombing carried out by the Royal Flying Corps. Every day and every night, on all our fronts, tons upon tons of bombs are dropped upon military positions behind the lines, sometimes so close as to be almost in the trench system and at other times fifty or sixty miles from our aerodromes. In order to carry out this work our machines have very often to literally fight their way to their destination and fight their way back again; but whatever opposition there may be the bombing is always carried out, and thus a continuous series of most vigorous and harassing blows are dealt the enemy's actual army in the field. No open town is ever bombarded, but only known submarine bases and, even then, only the actual naval works themselves.

The result of this continuous attention is that an incalculable amount of damage is caused to the enemy every day and every year, with the result that his efforts on the Front are seriously crippled and in any case rendered doubly difficult and perhaps ineffective in such a way that the lives of thousands of our soldiers are saved every month

And so there are the two pictures. The British Flying Corps directorate, happily too strong-minded to detach squadrons from the Front, where they are employed in a strict military sense, and dishonour its name with the acquirement of a sorry bag of German civilians, carries out its duties for the army in a clean but nevertheless tremendously effective manner. On the other hand, the German Flying Corps by a series of wholesale murders have not only deprived their soldiers of their services and of the services of the machines which might be built if they did not choose to spend months of valuable time constructing Zeppelins, but by their deeds dishonoured a name which they might have kept clean.

Well, if instead of carrying out their legitimate work against our army to the uttermost, the enemy prefers to cast his tarnished reputation upon even his air service, we are well content that they should continue in their imagined splendour.

However, despite the heavy work which a constantly increasing number of stunts per day occasioned, we all contrived to have a very jolly time, for not only did we have the usual gaps between flights but occasionally a merciful Providence saw fit to give us a spell of bad weather, when it was very much a case of a "For this relief, much thanks!"

The aerodrome was situated quite close to a French town of considerable size, and to this town we often repaired in a small body. Sometimes the flight would do the early morning and pre-lunch stunts and we would have our work done for the day by about 3 or 4 o'clock; the flight commander and his five pilots would then seize a vehicle of some description and waft themselves with the utmost rapidity to scenes less closely connected with the war.

A good many people, Americans particularly chaff us for our inordinate lust for that aromatic if unexciting beverage, tea, and we certainly must plead guilty to a distinct weakness in that direction; it was therefore only natural that the French should find this out and make the necessary arrangements for its gratification in exchange for our hard earned (?) *francs*. In our little town the purveyor was a very volatile young Frenchwoman rejoicing in the name of Alice—what her surname was I never knew—who had furnished a large parlour behind her father's butcher shop with little tables, a piano and a gramophone.

Into this palatial *salon* we would descend in a body, and in "pidgeon" French demand tea and cakes. Alice would then dive into a mysterious cupboard and produce large dishes of most succulent dainties, follow this up by large pots of excellent tea, and having thus won the hearts of the Englishmen in the usual manner—by feeding them—proceed to entertain the company by her voice, piano, and gramophone.

She had two stock songs, which by the time I left the Front I knew by heart, but nevertheless her intentions were good, and she did much to cheer the squadron up.

The gramophone was generally treated with the excellent policy of let sleeping dogs lie, but occasionally one of our Canadian pilots would loose it off and whirl the astonished but delighted Alice round in a fearsome fox-trot, the Englishmen, to their discredit, generally being too indifferent performers to essay such a feat

Conversation with Alice was a most exciting sport, as she knew little English and we less French, but despite these difficulties both sides understood each other perfectly, although the process was sometimes involved, to say the least! Contrariwise a good many of us had been badly "had" by the French by the way of language, in that one would stop outside a French shop and carefully rehearse one's little speech in French, by which one hoped to obtain what one wanted. Having got letter perfect one marched boldly in and painfully, with much labour, delivered one's short oration to the smiling proprietress; then, when one had completed a long request which had probably taken half an hour to concoct, she would reply in perfect English, "Oh, yes, sir, would you like ruled or plain paper?" or "Would you prefer thick or thin nibs, sir?" etc., etc., after which the highly embarrassed flying officer, blushing down past his chest protector, would mutter incoherently and flee!

After tea at Alice's we would generally meander back to the mess or else arrange a dinner in the little hotel If we chose the hotel we generally managed to obtain a jolly fine dinner, doubly interesting because one was never certain what one was going to get, except liquids, over which a Flying Corps officer can generally be relied upon as an expert! Ahem!

Our mess was situated in a large unfurnished *château*, adjacent to the aerodrome itself. In its empty rooms we erected our camp beds and generally spread ourselves out in as comfortable a manner as possible. The *château* had one charming adjunct in the shape of a perfectly good bathroom, which was inevitably the subject of many a grisly battle about priority between would-be users, but even so it was a boon which enabled us to look down from an infinite eminence on other squadrons who pigged it in small canvas baths.

The mess room itself was a nice long oak panelled room with a large fireplace at one end and equipped with the usual piano and gramophone, for which we constantly sent to England for fresh records.

After dinner each man would settle down to the kind of evening which pleased him best, some to write, some to read, some to play cards, and occasionally a gay spark would mysteriously disappear for the evening on business not unconnected with—er, steady chaps! Occasionally a curious paradox was presented by the sight of two aerial cutthroats, both wearing the ribbon of the Military Cross, playing—chess!

On some nights we entertained other squadrons, and then we really let ourselves go. A certain amount of caution always has to be observed in a jollification, for the extreme unpleasantness of the aftermath is greatly increased when one finds one's self reluctantly poised in the air with a splitting morning-after-the-night-before head, time 5 p. m., job, three hours' bomb raid! At such times one's chief worry is that one won't be shot down! But nevertheless, early morning stunt or not, we had some memorable times, but I don't think we ever reached the standard of some squadrons, especially those on the Somme.

I remember one curious and interesting evening which culminated in everyone being thrown out of the mess window, starting with the brigadier general, who was the guest of honour, and proceeding down through the wing commander, squadron commander and flight commanders to the most junior flying officers! The hosts, however, were the most considerate of men, for previous experience having provided them with data, they most thoughtfully stationed two of their officers outside the window to receive the guests and their own people as they came out. The brigadier, colonel and other senior officers were naturally the first to rush back and assist in the downfall of their projectors, so that all was square and above board and no one missed his share.

If someone were to write a book entitled *Nights in Flying Corps Messes* the reading of it would be wonderful!

Thank Heaven for this spirit of happy-go-lucky which is so often found in the Flying Corps for without it life at the Front would be unbearable!

Undoubtedly the hardest worked officer in our squadron was the equipment officer, who worked from early morning, before breakfast, until sometimes 10 or 11 o'clock at night. Responsible as he was of such a multitude of different matters—attending at one moment to the supply of a complete war machine, and the next to a new pair of breeches for one of the men; from the petrol supply to the quality of the meat for the men's dinners; for the safe upkeep of a large quantity of motor transport; and for quantities and quantities of things far too numerous to be mentioned.

Past military age and with therefore no obligation to serve at all, he slaved often far into the night in his efforts to maintain his organisation at the most highly strained point of efficiency.

There was not for him the excitement and glamour of fighting and destruction of Huns, but only a steady and monotonous grind of hard work.

He earned his pay!

Our hum-drum life was occasionally enlivened by the advent of fresh effort on the part of the Huns to prevent our various enterprises for his destruction, and the intensity of air fighting itself rose and fell with varying degrees of heat throughout our stay, but it never seriously interfered with any strafing project that came before our notice, and the daily Flying Corps *communiqués* were full of accounts of raids, machines driven down, hostile battery silenced and the like, and occasionally a short account of some exceptionally good show put up by some flying officer along the Front.

A friend of mine had a very interesting five minutes later on in the proceedings. He was flying in close formation just behind the leader when a machine swung straight across the latter's path. In order to clear it the leader had to make a violent turn and unfortunately crashed straight into my friend's machine. The leader's machine was smashed and hurled down to a fall in which he was killed. The second machine had part of its wings cut off and as a consequence began to fall in rapid circles, absolutely out of control

The observer immediately climbed out of his cockpit and crawled along one of the wings until he reached the tip, where he continued to cling on, his weight enabling the pilot to regain sufficient control to turn the machine west over our lines and effect a landing!

During all this time—the crash having occurred at five thousand feet—the observer gallantly stuck to his post, although both expected the machine to fall to pieces at any moment, and by his extraordinary coolness saved the whole situation, for which hair-raising performance he was afterward decorated

On another occasion—quite recently—one of our two-seater machines was badly hit and crashed almost into the German lines. The pilot and the observer extricated themselves while the wrecked machine was heavily shelled by the enemy, and swam some distance along a canal under heavy fire until they reached our front line, into which they successfully made their escape.

They afterwards objected strongly to being sent up in an aeroplane and then to complete their journey by swimming, an aquatic sport charming in itself but rather too exciting when undertaken in a heavy leather coat and boots and attended by painfully accurate Boche fire.

On another day one of our two-seater Armstrong machines was attacked by six Hun scouts who grouped themselves, two underneath, two over our machine, and one on either wing tip; they proceeded to fire hopefully into the Armstrong, the occupants of which returned the fire with equal hope, which was rapidly realised when they shot down one of the Huns in flames. This occasioned an immediate dispersal of the remaining five, and during the confusion the Armstrong successfully regained a safer locality!

I have previously remarked that it is necessary for machines to go over the lines grouped into formations in order to consolidate their offensive and defensive powers; and it is rare that machines ever cross the lines unless they are so grouped, the only exception being artillery machines. Therefore to stray from formation anywhere far from the lines is simply asking for trouble—a request which the Hun answers with surprising alacrity. A man may be flying along in the midst of information and be unable to discern a Hun anywhere in sight, yet if he strays from it a few minutes and gets separated from it by any distance he is immediately confronted by what appears to be the entire German Air Service.

So formations generally stick close together. But, nevertheless, an exception was provided by a member of one of our scout formations, composed of Nieuport and Morane scouts who were carrying out an offensive patrol far into an enemy country. This pilot drifted away from his comrades and suddenly found himself about a mile from them. At the same moment he caught sight of a formation of six large machines bearing down on him between him and his comrades. Instantly summing them up as a very fast two-seater German type which he knew, he tucked his tail between his legs, so to speak, and beetled back to his formation with every ounce of speed he could make, attended quite closely meanwhile by the six machines. Expecting to be the object of the concentrated fire from six pilots and six observers he spent a very unhappy period, until eventually regaining the rest of his flight, he ranged up to them with an enormous sigh of relief and turned round to look at the six Huns.

Judge his mortification when he saw six British Martinsyde bombers pass calmly by on their way back from a long distance bomb raid!

The poor wretch never heard the end of his marvellous escape from six of *our* machines.

Apart from Huns in the air we all had exhilarating moments some time or other at the hands of the faithful and most energetic Archie, who pursued us with his big black shell bursts with the greatest patience whenever we crossed over. True, his efforts were generally more frightening than damaging, but his shooting always showed a steady improvement, and he occasionally got a bull—

There was a very able Archie battery somewhere in La Bassée who gave us a very warm time occasionally, who was later joined by a very able confederate who lodged himself in a wood called the Bois de Biez, just above La Bassée, and the two of them were especially annoying. Rumour said that the new man was a specially imported marksman from the Somme, and I must admit that although he didn't make great hits, he successfully prevented any attempts at our making war languidly and peacefully.

His efforts so enraged one of our artillery squadrons that they determined to get their own back, and they accordingly deputed two of their people to go over and be Archied while two others tried to locate the gun flash—a difficult business, as the gun was sure to be well camouflaged. However, these four bright spirits discovered what they took to be Archie's whereabouts and commenced an artillery strafe on him.

He was shot at on and off for about three hours, the artillery sometimes just putting in a shell now and again in the hope of catching him unawares. During the whole of this time no single shell disturbed any of the machines in that region, as the revengeful squadron was also having a little interview with the gentleman at La Bassée at the same time.

Both these anti-aircraft batteries had been by this time pretty well plastered, and eventually the ranging machine, chortling with glee, concluded that they were done for. The pilot went down to about two thousand above the Bois de Biez, and did three triumphant loops over his fallen enemy, and then went down to La Bassée and did three more, finally coming back to tell the glad news of Archie's downfall.

A quarter of an hour after he disappeared, both Archies burst into full and healthy song, and gave some of our fellows quite a warm time!

The artillery squadron that evening had to put up with the telephonic inquiries of about eight other squadrons as to whether they could loan them a real artillery observer to settle the Archies!

I had chanced to be up myself with another man that morning and had seen a lonely two-seater of ours flying up and down high over these two batteries. He was having the most peaceful time, for neither of the batteries shot at him and he was left undisturbed to wander about and carry on his lawful trade, which was probably photography. We thought that we should cheer him up tremendously if we went over to him, just to show him that the scouts knew he was there and looking after him, and so on. We accordingly crossed the lines and flew right up to him and circled round waving our hands.

Just at this moment we were assaulted by a furious storm of shell bursts, the two Archies below, evidently considering that they now had a target worth shooting at! Bethinking ourselves of more sylvan resorts we hurriedly retired from the scene, and then turned round to look at our handiwork. The wretched two-seater was now madly stunting about in a perfect sea of black puffs as the energetic Archie, whom we had stirred up, set to his work. The poor devil of a two-seater, having his job complete, had to stay there and enjoy the proceedings as best it could, while we, its brave protectors, proceeded on our accustomed beat!

These two anti-aircraft batteries provided us with a great deal of interest and were responsible for some very humorous happenings. They grew very cunning eventually and matters resolved themselves into a sort of chess game between us. The flight commander, a very seasoned dodger, delighted to go over and draw their fire and then carry out a series of well thought out manoeuvres, with the consequence that in about two minutes Archie's bursts were nearly a quarter of a mile away from him!

When he had finished with them he used to throw a loop or two and retire from their society for the morning, probably leaving the gun crews gnashing their teeth in true Teutonic mortification! As a counter blast to our efforts to dodge him Archie brought in quite a number of clever ideas, especially in respect to ranging, but the Flying Corps rapidly learned them as he produced them and altered its methods to suit. A favourite trick of the wily gunners was to wait till one of our machines had crossed back over the lines on its way home, and was flying unsuspectingly in a straight course, when he would loose off a spasm of most rapid fire in the hope of catching the machine before it could dodge. In this way he put quite a shower of shrapnel bullets through the tank of a machine we were escorting, but happily the bullet holes were all above the petrol level, and as the petrol was fed by gravity no harm was done, although the pilot's nerves received quite a jar, as the shell burst between his wing tip and his tail, which as he remarked, "Was too close to be blooming well pleasant!"

The weather sometimes played us dirty tricks by getting bad suddenly while we were up over the lines, so that we had great difficulty in regaining our aerodrome, particularly in regard to mists.

One afternoon the weather suddenly turned very cloudy and misty, with the result that lots of people had anxious times getting home. One interesting instance was provided by a bright youth who was caught by the mists very low down a long way east of the lines.

He immediately set off westward and flew on, until he was overjoyed to see a large working party which he instantly summed up as being German prisoners working under our guard As he badly wanted information as to what direction his aerodrome lay he selected a field near the working party and landed in it, but kept his engine running very slowly.

A French peasant quickly made his appearance and ran up to the side of his machine. The pilot at once asked him:

"Where is ——?" (The name of his aerodrome.)

The peasant looked very puzzled and shook his head.

The pilot repeated his question.

The peasant replied that he didn't know.

The pilot then asked the peasant "In what direction are the lines?"

The peasant pointed—*west!*

The horror-stricken pilot instantly realised that, being further from the lines than he thought, he had landed well on the German side! Without further parley he threw open his throttle and took the machine off, leaving the mystified peasant still wondering at the mad *pilote-aviateur*. The German prisoners, far from being prisoners, were in reality a strong fatigue party!

Continuing his flight he once more headed westward, the weather in the meantime having become very thick indeed. After flying for a long time he came upon a town and circled low down over the middle of it. He was immediately greeted by a heavy rifle and machine fire, and discerned numbers of grey uniformed figures running about over the streets. This reception assured him over whose territory he was, and he pushed on once again through the mists, intending to fly west until there was no more petrol. After further adventures he eventually landed a few miles our side of the lines, with his petrol supply absolutely exhausted, having spent anything but a dull afternoon!

A sudden fog or mist is the bane of an aviator's life, for if caught up in the air in a fog his position is really desperate, especially at the Front, for there the wind, coming, as it generally seems to, from the west, prevents him flying with the wind, overhauling the fog bank, and landing in clear weather ahead of it, because if he did so he would naturally land in German territory. He is therefore faced with the unhappy alternative of either plunging down at once or flying about until his petrol exhausts and then dropping wherever he happens to be, either of which alternatives are perfectly beastly and highly dangerous. Sometimes a fog bank will closely hug the ground and leave the tops of tall trees visible, like masts sticking out of the sea. Here again a pilot can be badly taken in, for if be selects a place where he can see no tree tops and tries to get down, he probably finds himself crashing into the middle of a small village.

A certain flight commander, returning from an early morning bomb raid, was caught by a thick mist which had blown up from the west since he had started, and which had already blown over the lines. After a time he came down very low and flew along just on top of the mist looking for a possible clear space. He explained the occurrence to me thus:

> I was flying along very low over the mist, and both the observer and I were looking for a thin place in it so that we might get a glimpse of the ground. I was looking over myself very intently, when the next second a nurse helped me to sit up in bed and drink some hot gravy beef!

The lapse of time between looking at the mist and drinking the gravy beef had been nearly two days, but he knew nothing of it! His observer was badly injured, but they both got over it and made splendid recoveries, although their noses were ever afterwards somewhat different shapes!

Our pilots represented the most cosmopolitan body of men of, I should imagine, any unit of the British Army. Ghanaians, Australians, South Africans, Irishmen, Scotchmen, and numerous Englishmen who had lived or travelled in far corners of the world made up our personnel. Sometimes of an evening they would all sit down and tell lies to each other about their respective abodes, while we untravelled people gazed in astonishment, and made resolves to go to a fresh country almost every night, according to whom we had been talking to during the evening!

In the mess, in our sports, and in the air, let it suffice to say that they were at all times and in every sense, gentlemen, chivalrous and courageous to a degree which rendered the squadron as happy a unit as any on the Front.

The men also provided wonderful samples of versatility, for all kinds of trades and all grades of society were represented. If one's wrist watch wanted repair one merely approached the technical sergeant major, who instantly provided an expert watch maker, who, if clad in the uniform of a second class mechanic, lacked nothing in technical skill; with the result that after a brief period, during which the air mechanic probably asked for leave to go into the town to buy some material, one's watch came back once more in perfect order. Or perhaps one decided that a tunic wanted some sweeping alteration; a few inquiries, and a master tailor appeared, probably masquerading as a wing coverer, who, producing from some mysterious source a cigar box containing the implements of his trade, begged the loan of one's table, and effected the alteration as skilfully as any West-end tailor.

Perhaps one was foolish enough to mess about with the mathematical side of an aeroplane's design, just for amusement, and getting all messed up, go about crying for assistance, which would probably be immediately forthcoming in the shape of some individual with a bulging forehead, to whom the nth calculus was a mere flea bite, but who normally followed the occupation of splicing wire and control cables!

Newcoming officers were naturally the object of very keen and critical observation from the rest of the pilots, and their methods of flying, discipline and general character held up to a very keen analysis. Sometimes, being perhaps a trifle unused to our special type of scout, they did not fly so well—a failing which was very rapidly made good after a few hours' air experience. Sometimes, for a little carelessness, inexperience, and bad judgment, they crashed, landing, with the result that they were either despatched away to the aircraft depot for a new machine or that the mechanics in their flight worked all night long to repair the machine and have it serviceable in the morning, according to the gravity of the crash.

Occasionally their ideas about punctuality and the responsibility of a pilot were a trifle ephemeral, but in a week or so they found their feet and became steady and reliable, and whatever their initial shortcomings were they were never lacking in the *sine qua non* of an officer—the quality with which these junior officers have done so much to place the Royal Flying Corps on the right of the line of the army, with His Majesty the King as Colonel in Chief—personal courage.

It is the close of a long autumn day during which many stunts have been successfully pulled off. The squadron has escorted three bomb raids and done six offensive patrols—a gruelling day's work. Three of the enemy's machines have been accounted for, and somewhere out in the darkening east two of our pilots are missing.

Dinner is over, and the officers are sitting in the front rows of seats listening to a squadron concert which is being held in a large canvas hangar. One canvas wall has been rolled up for ventilation, and as we sit we can look out to the west, where our eyes see the last soft crimson glow fade into a delicate faint blue, then darker, and then to star set blackness over our heads. All along the eastern horizon there is the constant rising and falling flicker of star shells; and the audience, clad in oily khaki, sitting in deadly silence, can hear the eternal solemn roll and mutter of the guns, while another demonstrator of the squadron's versatility, a youthful air mechanic, still rather oily and tired with the day's work, is singing with a voice like an angel:

—to the end of a perfect day.

CHAPTER 12

Zep Strafing

The far end of the aerodrome, even when the moon was not obscured, was lost in the faint shadowy wreaths of grey mist which overhung the low, flat countryside of Essex. From the big hedge skirting the edge of the landing place the ground ran up, a grey moisture laden piece of grass, till it culminated in the shallow morass of mud which surrounded the hangars, which raised themselves black and silent from the wet earth, and lay, a gloomy silhouette, against the sky. Behind them, barely visible, were two low masses—the men's barracks—in the shape of two long wooden huts. About two hundred yards from the barracks was a smaller building, which served half as an orderly room and half as an officers' mess. Some officers' quarters, store houses, and one or two tents completed the camp.

All windows and openings were carefully shuttered, in a way which brought joy to a number of well meaning and elderly gentlemen, who, after a busy day in the City, donned armlet and truncheon and became most ubiquitous special constables, whose duty it was to prevent any promiscuous illumination which might tend to be (theoretically) of assistance to the patient Boche, who, mounted in expensive Zeppelins, endeavoured to destroy London with a lack of success which must have sorely tried even Teutonic patience and thoroughness.

In the interior of one of the barracks, a piano, gramophone, and several raucous cockney voices battled for the mastery, but happily the stout walls of the hut thinned the result down considerably, to every one's satisfaction!

The big sheets of canvas forming the front doors of the hangars rustled dismally in a chilly breeze, punctuated by a melancholy drip, drip, of moisture falling from the wet roof into puddles round the walls. It had been raining with the true persistency of English weather for two days, and had only stopped about three hours before, and now the pungent smell of wet ground and dank air, combined with the chilly infinity of countryside spread around in a veritable blackness of Tartarus, gave an overwhelming sense of sombre dreariness.

The flight commander turned on his heel and shouted into the darkness.

"Flight Sergeant!"

An answering "Yes, sir," rang out from the vicinity of the orderly room, followed by the sound of someone ploughing their way through the mud.

A dark figure ranged up to the commander and saluted.

"Flight Sergeant, what do you think of things tonight?"

The figure eyed the sky before replying.

It was not very clear, and the weak moonlight was constantly obscured by the passing volumes of flaccid, low-lying *cumulus*, crowding together into great banks as the main mass broke and dispersed.

"Well, it's a horrible night, although it's clearing up a bit, but I don't think it's very good for *them*, do you, sir?"

"Oh, it's beastly enough in all conscience, but I think that this stuff's going to break up a good deal yet, and it mightn't be so bad before midnight, except for this cursed mist. Anyway, have the flares put out right away, ready to light, will you, Flight Sergeant?"

"Very good, sir."

He bustled off and routed out about half a dozen of the musical *dilettantes*, who presently, with much caustic and flowery comment on the state of their native element, squelched noisily through it out into the mist and placed petrol flares in their proper positions ready to be lit in case any hostile frightfulness occasioned the ascent of a machine.

This job having been done to the complete satisfaction of the flight sergeant, the party was immediately swallowed up by their wooden den, from whence sweet strains once more resumed their full throated, if unmelodious, chorus.

The flight commander endeavoured to pick the driest course through the mud towards the mess, but presently threw caution to the winds and swam boldly on, with a painful lack of consideration for the feelings of the long suffering mortal who cleaned his boots. He paused on the doorstep and peered London-wards for a moment.

The great city, although not far off, gave no hint of its presence. In the middle of it, not a thousand miles from Hyde Park, lived his wife;

a fact which considerably added to his already sincere wish that the night would remain too bad for air raids.

He opened the door and stepped into a snug little room, comfortably "fuggy" with the efforts of a large black stove, round which sprawled half a dozen flying officers in various comfortable positions of after dinner boa constriction. Their wicker chairs creaked as they twisted round to look at him.

"Hallo, Palser! '*Oh, Watchman, what of the nigh*'?"

"Oh, pretty poisonous, but clearing up. It's not unlikely that there will be dirty work at the cross roads tonight!"

A chorus of groans answered him.

"But, my dear old bean, you couldn't see your own tail in this mist!"

"I know. That's why there'll be dirty work at the aforesaid thoroughfare junction!"

Another recumbent figure broke into speech.

"Well, if the Hun's any sort of a gentleman, he'll sit tight in his *biergarten* and leave us in peace until he gets a better night."

The perpetrator of a particularly thick cloud of tobacco smoke, lazily removing his pipe from his mouth, answered the hopeful one.

"But he isn't, you young ass. This is just the sort of night he likes to injure us hated English! Probably quite a few stray dogs, hens, and the usual quota of infants will fill his bag tonight. Where's your wife, Palser?"

"In town."

"So is mine, damn it!"

A short silence followed and then the cynical one started again.

"Remember that night when we got strafed in the potato field. Palser?"

"By Jove, yes! That was dashed funny."

"What's this about?" queried one of the newer pilots.

"Why, the old Hun came rattling over in his gas bag to England, way up the East Coast, when I was stationed up there. One of our fellows had a topping idea, which was put into effect. A great big potato field in a lonely bit of countryside was fitted out with a nice set of landing flares, which were lit on the approach of the Zeppelin. The dear old thing immediately concluded that it was a nice big aerodrome, caught on the hop with its flares still showing! He promptly loosed off his entire stock of unpleasantness. The net result was that several hundredweights of perfectly good potatoes were irretrievably ruined, after which the Hun, proud in the knowledge that a deadly blow had been struck for the Fatherland, beetled off home again!

"It's an awful shame that the whole affair wasn't published in the newspapers, for I think the ridicule would have penetrated even the Hun's thick head."

The merriment having subsided, Palser suggested a game of poker, to which all acquiesced.

About an hour later the game was rudely interrupted by the clang of the telephone bell.

A look of comprehension dawned in every eye;

"I told you so!" exclaimed Palser, as he reached for the telephone.

"Yes, sir, Captain Palser speaking."

A pause, while the expectant party watched the face of the flight commander as he listened to the headquarters.

"Very good then, sir. I'll see to it. Goodbye."

He put the telephone back on its shelf.

"Raiding Zeppelins expected over the coast in another hour, gentlemen."

A dead silence settled on the group while the flight commander rang for the flight sergeant, who, appearing a few minutes later, saluted smartly and stood stiffly to attention.

"Flight Sergeant, a raid expected. Run out Number 602 ready for me, and test the engine yourself, will you? And see every thing's O.K. I tested the gun earlier on, so that's all right Oh—as you go down tell my servant to get my flying kit from my room and put it in the machine."

"Yes, sir!" responded the flight sergeant, and turned away to carry out his orders.

The flight commander went to the door, looked out, and came back to the card table.

"Weather much the same—few good clouds and still misty. Sweet night for a flip! I'd love to have one of those extremely puissant what-are-the-Flying-Corps-doing agitators in the front seat tonight!"

Speculation became general while the flight waited for fresh news. After a while the inconsiderate telephone rang again.

"Yes, sir. A signal! Take this down, one of you."

One of the party scribbled out the message as the flight commander repeated it.

Hostile aircraft crossing East Coast proceeding towards London at approximately twelve thousand feet. Use own discretion reference weather, but send up machine if possible.' Sender's initials. Righto. Captain Palser receiving! Goodbye."

"We don't get much, but we do see life," sighed the flight commander as he made for the door. "Think of all the other poor blighters around London who are getting the same signal! I'm going up in 602, Harry, so sit by the phone and listen to headquarters; if they want another machine you had better go up yourself. Bye-bye."

He stumbled out into the darkness which, after the electric light, seemed more Tartarus-like than ever. From the direction of London great glaring pencils of light reached up to the sky, searching it minutely.

The searchlights were taking no chances!

Sounds of revelry in the barracks had ceased, for the mechanics were "standing to" at their posts. As he came up to his faithful two-seater—faithful on many a previous night's adventure—the flight sergeant turned round and saluted him.

"Machine O. K. and engine perfect, sir. Shall I have the flares lit, sir?"

"Yes, at once, Flight Sergeant." He gave a quick look into the empty front seat—empty because weight tells in a long climb, and a minute may mean the loss of a splendid opportunity. While he was getting in his machine a number of mechanics ran out to light up the big petrol flares which were arranged to light the aerodrome sufficiently for him to get off.

He switched on the instrument board lighting set and began to buckle the belt.

"This gun hasn't been touched since I tested it, has it?"

"No, sir."

His mechanic, standing beside the propeller, now called back to him.

"Switch off, petrol on, air closed, sir?"

He repeated the words as he complied. Then:

"Contact, sir!"

"Contact."

The mechanic gave the propeller a strong swing round, but the engine did not start.

"Huh, she's jolly cold!" muttered Palser. "Give her another swing. Smith."

The mechanic did, and the engine started. Then the engine was tested "all out" while Palser intently watched the tachometer dial Then he throttled down and turned to the flight sergeant, who was standing beside the cockpit

"She's all right. I'll push off if the flares are all lit?"

"They are, and the men are back, sir. And the best of luck to you, sir!"

Palser waved "chocks away," pulled his goggles down over his eyes, and opened the throttle. The powerful engine drew the machine quicker and quicker over the ground and he was flying by the time he shot by the last flare.

His main anxiety was to hold the machine dead straight until he was well away from the ground, for unless the night is very clear, even an experienced pilot has to be most careful in this respect, as an aviator normally preserves his balance by comparison with the earth, mainly by sense of sight. At night, and when all lights on the ground are extinguished, equilibrium becomes a matter of no small difficulty, particularly if there be clouds obscuring the stars.

He soon began a wide circle over the aerodrome as the landing flares kept him informed of his position, and he intended to get fairly high before leaving its vicinity. He knew the country round about like a book, and even in the dark could guess his way with a fair amount of accuracy, which in itself was an extraordinary asset to a night flyer.

He settled back in his seat and tried to relax his mind and muscles as much as possible, while the machine made its long climb skyward.

But tonight he found it difficult. He could not relax For some time past his piloting had told him that he had been flying too long—far too long. Ten hectic months on the Western Front followed by months of nearly continuous night flying, had shaken his originally iron nerve almost to pieces, and now, for all his efforts to the contrary, he found himself sitting up tensely in his machine, every nerve and muscle strained to breaking point.

It was not fear. His highly strung imagination had long ago faced and defeated that dread spectre which suggests to men that they will be afraid—cowards. No, he was not afraid, but—yet his nerves jarred and jangled at the slightest cause.

He remembered moodily how, only the previous afternoon, while having tea with his wife, he had jumped clean out of his chair at the sound of a maid's knuckle, rapping at the door—so like a machine gun.

"By Gad, if I get down from this I'll apply for a month's leave tomorrow. They have offered it to me twice, and I'm not going to refuse any longer. Dash it! I am like a blessed child in the air, and I'd better stop before I crash myself to blazes—"

He had been speaking aloud, while the sound of his voice was cut off and blown back past his fur lined helmet The sound of his own voice had been companionable for a moment, but now there only remained the unnoticed drone of engine and wind as they swayed on in the vast vault of blackness.

In the darkness there was no sense of speed, but only that of overpowering loneliness. Now, far below him, the landing flares were a little indistinct shimmer of light, occasionally obliterated by a rolling wave of mist, grey topped in the weak moonlight Sometimes he skirted a cloud and experienced the momentary realisation of his terrific speed. Then it fell away behind him and he was once more left as if motionless in a high wind.

The subdued illumination of the tiny electrics was reflected back to him by the white enamelled dial faces, which threw eerie shadows around the cockpit.

Impassive, unwinking, they mocked him with their details of speed and height. The altimeter was showing him that he was now over ten thousand feet from the earth, alone—if he fainted, what a drop. Yes, he was far from help—ten thousand feet—alone—alone

He sat up and cursed savagely to himself. His imagination was running wild with him. He hurled the machine around with a strong wrench at the controls and set off towards the searchlights, and diverted his attention to watching the sky where they groped for the enemy he was up to destroy.

But their ceaseless sweep showed nothing but fragments of cloud.

He turned disappointedly east and flew down the river, and then north again in a fruitless search. Bound again once more, in a long reach to the southward.

Then an inexplicable sense of expectation led him to turn and gaze to the north again.

Yes!

A number of searchlight beams were concentrated to a spot far away to the north, and about his own level. A second or two later, brilliant red flashes dotted the sky with an inferno of bursting shrapnel around a long, slim, silver cigar.

He turned and hurried northwards at his utmost speed with the throttle wide open, meanwhile anxiously watching the scene in front of him.

A black speck, like an overgrown fly, suddenly burst into the columns of light and made for the Zeppelin.

One of our machines was attacking.

The shrapnel bursts died away as if by magic, while the speck and the cigar raced on through the night, implacably followed by the white arms of the searchlights.

Then a needle of brilliant flame connected the aeroplane and the Zeppelin. Our machine was pouring in heavy machine gun fire.

Palser, breathing faster and faster as he watched the strange duel, that he was too far away to take part in, raced on.

Suddenly the end of the cigar began to glow. The glow burst into long yellow streams of flame, and the great Zeppelin, tilting up on one end, began to drop.

Now the flames were extending its whole length. Palser pictured the wretched crew, confronted with an awful death by burning or suicide by jumping into the void, and shivered.

Then the two ends of the Zeppelin folded up, and she fell, a streak of brilliant flame in her long dreadful drop to—Ugh! What more awful death!

It was over.

Palser gave a long sigh and sank back into his cockpit, but he could not rid himself of the picture of the crew on the stricken airship, faced with their terrible alternative.

He flew about for another hour but nothing more met his eye, so he began the homeward journey.

He was longing to get down, for he felt that he had come to the limit of his capacity. Once or twice already he had possessed a fleeting doubt as to whether he could keep control of himself until the end of his patrol, and felt it strange that he should have suddenly reached this queer state, but nevertheless it had to be accepted.

He throttled down and commenced his long glide earthwards.

Then his whole senses were stricken by a pounding blow of realisation, which left his whole being chilled like ice.

For in the front seat, his head and shoulders faintly but distinctly visible in odd reflections from the instrument lights, *sat an observer!*

He leaned forward and gazed with horror at the strange passenger, while a chilling terror crept into his heart A *passenger!* God! What *was* it?

But still it sat perfectly immobile, its leather helmet gleaming faintly.

He shouted a question across but it neither moved nor answered. He strove desperately to pull himself together. He *knew* that he had not brought a passenger, but yet—was he going mad? What awful insanity was gripping him? He tried to read the instrument dials but they were only a blur. He was leaning on the stick and the machine was diving wildly down, but he did not notice it.

He strained forward again. *It* was still there.

But slowly, as if with infinite pain, its head began to turn.

His overtired brain shuddered within itself; what will its face be?

He heard his own roar of insane laughter. His brain had gone then! Mad! The machine swung in great circles. He was just collecting enough to know that he had dashed into a great cloud. Earth and sky were blotted out on both sides with the rushing grey fog.

He vainly tried to right the machine. He did not know whether he was upside down, or how. Then there started the dreaded spinning nose dive.

The hateful head still confronting him, he plunged into the seemingly bottomless pit of space—spinning, spinning—until—*cra*—*ash!*

A miraculous escape—two broken legs and an arm.

An unconscious, bleeding figure, found alone in a mess of wreckage.

Hallucination—nerves—or—?

Chapter 13

The Somme

One night in the late autumn one of the machines was forced by engine trouble to land comparatively close up to the trenches. As the machine was more or less intact a party was despatched from the aerodrome to dismantle it and bring it back. The map reference given up over the telephone showed its position to be some considerable distance away towards the southern end of our patrol, and consequently the journey took so long that it was not until just after dusk that we found it. The job proved to be a fairly long one as the machine had to be pulled by hand over some pretty rough country to a spot where working lights were not so likely to be visible to the enemy. Then the machine had to be completely dismantled, practically in the darkness, for the party, not possessing the *savoir faire* of the infantry and other troops, who frequent muddy burrows for months on end, did not dare to show a light in the direction of the enemy.

Throughout the long night the sights, and particularly the sounds, just behind the lines were very interesting, and, despite the fact that no human beings could be seen or directly heard, these sounds gave an impression of a tremendous activity going on. The Very's lights lit up the lines with an eerie bluish flicker, sometimes increased to a glare when numbers were fired off together. Odd rifle shots fired off here and there, occasionally swelling to a burst of rapid fire, then dying away again, the rapid chatter of a machine gun, followed by unearthly silence. The *swi—i—ish, bomp* of an occasional shell, sometimes swelling into a miniature strafe.

The sounds pictured in the mind's eye, as nothing else would have, an impression of the various enterprises being stealthily carried out, the adequacy of the same being sometimes well advertised by the peaceful silence which prevailed in certain sectors. Yet sooner or later some of these sectors would be lit up brilliantly by whole salvoes of star shells, or Very's lights, and a machine gun or two would begin to snap and stutter with deadly intensity.

It did not require a great effort of the imagination to conceive that somebody's working party, or an attempted raid, had been discovered by a watchful sentry. A rush of lights, a machine gun chorus, the snicker of rifle fire, a dozen or so of shells, and that a darkness and silence more eloquent than words; a darkness which lowered down again over the sea of muddy wire and mangled corpses, while the less mangled tried to crawl their painful way back to their trenches.

In the foreground the pale moon lit up white piles of ruins—all that was left of a stricken hamlet—the leafless, branchless trees, all shot about and scarred by the past three years of flying steel, often hung with the little telephone wires that wended their way eastward, and disappeared into the black mysterious unknown land of mud, wire and death in front. Over all there brooded the same spirit that seemed apparent from the air—the spirit of frightful malignancy.

But the noises were after all only occasional. The line was then considered very "quiet." The noises were so occasional that they could be easily defined and their origin accurately placed; there were spells of a quite recognisable silence; yet not so far away things were so completely opposite as to shock the senses into an awed wonder.

Down on the southern horizon there spread a great mass of dancing, shivering but yet continuous light; such as might be the reflection of the burning of a great city, with every house alight. Hour after hour the crimson yellow fire glowed and swayed and lit the horizon with an unearthly glare; a glare which never perceptibly rose or fell but always remained intense. And to the ears there came the sound as of a mighty, hurricane-driven sea, angrily beating and battering some vast sea wall of hollow metal; the sound chord never rose or fell—a new and supplementary note might creep in, as the treble against the base, and disappear again—but shuddered the air with one incessant, implacable, earth-quivering roar. From dusk until just before dawn, when we left, the glare and the roar never stopped nor ever altered one iota, but persisted with a monotony that was maddening.

It was too terrific, too tremendous to grasp. It was terrible.

It was the Battle of the Somme!

From the clouds the Somme was equally staggering. The air itself seemed literally blocked with machines, and hundred upon hundreds could be counted anywhere around, of all types, speeds and sizes, and performing all descriptions of work.

Over the trenches and just inside them were whole crowds of our artillery machines working at all heights. Further in were the bombing squadrons going to and returning from their appointed strafing.. Long range artillery, photographic and reconnaissance machines dotted the sky in great numbers all over the place, and amongst, underneath and thousands of feet above there swarmed formation after formation of our fighting scouts. Close to the lines these scouts were not so apparent; instead there were the artillery ranging machines pursuing their calling in comparative peace except for Archie, further in there appeared more scouts until about five miles from the lines the main body came into view, body of really colossal size, forming as it did an aerial barrage between the Hun machines and the battle front

West of that belt the Hun was scarcely ever seen, and if he was seen he became the target of every machine in sight and was inevitably driven down.

This much for an enemy scout, while as for an artillery machine—it simply hadn't a ghost of a chance: If one ever did succeed in starting its wireless artillery control it probably completed its first signal in Hades so quickly that it scarcely knew what hit it!

All the fighting was taking place between three and five miles from the lines. Closer than that it was impossible for an enemy formation to approach without being forced either to flee before or fight one of our own offensive patrols. When this happened the fur began to fly in an appalling manner, but however much it flew the Huns did not get past. That they failed was not in many cases for the want of trying, for their scout formations very often displayed the greatest determination and courage to break through and smash up our artillery observation machines, and thus air fighting on the Somme was most extraordinary and fierce.

This was especially so about Bapaume, then in German hands, over and behind which a great number of highly interesting and to both sides instructive scraps took place.

The whole story of the air work and the fighting in the air which took place on the Somme Front is too vast and rambling to place accurately which was its rise and which was its zenith, while the various phases of the corps' work were prosecuted a hundred fold and even extended into branches of entirely new Hun strafing, but the fact remains that Flying Corps work increased enormously, and fighting became bitter in a war that more than transcended our previous experience. Both sides concentrated huge quantities of aircraft on the Front and every "Archie" battery that could be spared was brought down and massed into an organisation which by reason of the tremendous practice it had at our numerous formations, naturally became exceedingly annoying, and undoubtedly rendered those "moments of intense terror" which punctuate the boredom of war, more frequent!

The ground itself presented the most extraordinary sight conceivable. The front lines themselves were difficult to recognise, because every square foot of the surrounding earth had been churned up and pounded into a jelly by weeks of intense artillery preparation and trench barrage fire, until the rim of every shell hole ran into the rim of another, and left merely a great pitted sea of mud, through which straggled the nearly indefinable trenches themselves, even those losing their continuity in some great mine crater.

The shell pitted area extending back a distance which compared with the rest of the Front was most abnormal, as a result of the almost continuous barrage or curtain fire which was directed at the rear lines and communication trenches in order to prevent the enemy from bringing up stores and reinforcements, while various objects of interest—Miraumont Farm, Beaumont Hamel, Grandcourt, Martinpuich, Ginchy, Guillemont, Combles, Trones Wood—had been blotted out of all semblance of their original state and survived only as names, as stretches' of mud and stones rather deeper and more shell-torn than all the other mud; messes of broken stones and riven trees which once had been villages and woods, but which now, as I have said, had left only a name, the very application of which was grimly humorous. All over the ground, chiefly concentrating on trenches and trench works themselves, were dotted great lines and dusters of shell bursts, so incessant that the smoke formed great rolling banks which drifted away in almost unbroken sequence from the targets.

Flying low the view obtained of the German front line being "prepared" for the infantry attack was more than sufficient to give rise to the supposition that the war was over, that nothing could possibly survive—that we should walk through. Every yard of the gaping ditch called a trench was hidden every few seconds by the brilliant flash and ball of smoke from a bursting shell, their once protective parapets and parados being blown to powder into the gloomy pall which overhung the hiding places of the wretched enemy. Nor was this fire by any means promiscuously aimed, but could be clearly seen as directed against a recognisable target, on and around which the shell bursts were most accurately placed, thanks to a careful registration and the continual ranging of the artillery machines. On both sides of the lines great hosts of "crumps" steadily beat the ground day and night, culminating in a particular hell of steel along the opposing front lines. The artillery alone was so cruel and remorseless in its almost unbelievable volume that it momentarily wafted the rest of the Front into oblivion and made the latter seem almost futile.

In the stricken country intersected by trenches there was naturally no sign of life, but a comparatively short distance back the activity was truly remarkable, and the country was simply teeming with all the paraphernalia of the aggressors. In little clefts, hollows and folds in the ground were stationed very often large quantities of infantry with a disrespect for secrecy which quite shocked people used to the more retiring methods obtaining along the rest of the line. These troops were waiting their turn to debouch into one or other of the great arteries of communication trenches running up to the reserve lines; the same communication trenches viewed from a low altitude, generally appeared to possess a great amount of traffic, while during an actual assault troops moved backwards and forwards with the most *blasé* disregard of trenches and shell fire, philosophically reflecting with great perspicacity that the enemy artillery was far too engrossed in other efforts to prevent our success. A little further back still and everyone strolled about quite freely with more disregard than ever.

Sir Douglas Haig had said something about winning if the guns were placed "hub to hub" along the Front; here they were not only hub to hub, but line behind line, so closely set that the foremost but narrowly escaped the blasts of the rear lines. In one small field alone there were parked three whole batteries, the first one absolutely wheel to wheel at the eastern and of the field, the second one in the middle and the third one at the western end of the field, the two front lines having back protection against the blast of each other's guns. Neither was the case isolated, but typical of the terrific artillery concentration which was so evident everywhere.

Great heaps of shell cases littered the ground around the guns where the fire had been so rapid that the transport had not been able to keep up with the loads it had to carry back.

During a show itself, these batteries very often came into action under heavy fire and took up the positions they wanted right in the face of the enemy and streams of shells, making their motto very much "*business as usual,*" and although, sad to say, many a battery went under new management, it never failed to solicit a "continuation of patronage from our numbers of well pleased clients!"

Another peculiarity of the artillery was that it apparently had discovered the secret of perpetual motion, for it appeared to fire all the morning, all the afternoon and all night, each and every battery: and withal the gunners themselves were feeling rather well, a condition well understandable in view of their now inexhaustible supply of shells, guns, gunners, and tempting targets, with the result that they applied the first and last to each other with a blithesome zeal that astounded the tin-hatted Hindenburg hordes whom an obviously *unkultured* necessity made the unwilling recipients.

One had a passing wonder that the All Highest did not immediately make better arrangements with his friend *Gott*, or that he restrained his impetuous, all-conquering legions from leaping from their muddy dugouts (quite forty foot deep and lined with concrete) and staining their supermen's bayonets (as fitted with saw) with our *infidel* blood. One could only suppose that they considered that they considered their noble steel too honourable to stain with our plebeian gore. It must have been an oversight, for the obsession which so many people suffered from that the myriads of Attilas were prevented from coming over by our artillery, men, machine guns and aeroplanes, was obviously too absurd to be even considered....

However...

Everywhere back four or five miles from the lines the country swarmed with transports and troops, the roads themselves having soon become inadequate for the traffic with the result that it appeared to travel to a great extent across country. Everywhere in sight huge clouds of dust overspread the crowded ground as convoy after convoy of motor transport wended its way to and from the front, interspersed with bodies of cavalry, artillery, Army Service Corps, horsed wagons, ambulances and most of all the individuals who were to take the leading part and for whom all the rest was destined to assist: the infantry.

All over the ground occupied by what appeared to be a sort of mammoth world's fair were pieces of more or less smooth and open ground—aerodromes. Here again numbers were astonishing. One could flop down most anywhere and hit an aerodrome of some sort—an aerodrome, too, populated by numbers of most ardent people to whom business was business, and who had a great pride in their game book, officially styled as the *Combat Report Record*. In these interesting volumes were the details of the daily bag of Huns, each entry being a brief description of why and how the Hun got his name there. As the preserves were well stocked and the sportsmen fine shots, it got fatter and fatter in a most pleasant manner.

Some of the most remarkable flying in the world was to be seen daily around these aerodromes, chiefly among the fighting scouts, the pilots of which stunted their machines about in a bloodcurdling variety of tricks, one squadron in particular taking a great joy in performing a vertical bank between rugby goal posts with the cross bar removed, their wing tip about two feet from the ground, and playing catch-as-catch-can with each other around the hangars, to the greatest terror to everyone but themselves.

Which reminds me of the case of a well known pilot who delighted to fly right through a large shed at one of our big aerodromes. The shed was very big and he used to constantly fly in one end and out the other, a feat demanding a certain amount of judgment, as there was not much room between his wing tips and the wall. All went well and the performance was greatly admired by everyone except the mechanics in the shed, until one day, entering one end of the shed at a little over one hundred miles an hour, he discovered that the door at the other end was shut.

His only remark as the various chunks were sewn together again was: "I knew that some damn fool would leave that door shut!"

The morale of the pilots was very "uppish" and each one thought himself capable of settling at least six Huns at once, single handed, a belief not altogether unjustified by actuality. In connection with this a rather curious case was the adventure of one of our pilots flying a De Havilland pusher scout. This machine possessed a gun which the pilot nearly always kept pointing straight ahead; the mounting itself was fixed to one of two vertical tubes sliding on each other so that it could be raised and lowered considerably at will. Flying this machine some distance from the lines and for some unaccountable reason alone, our pilot was suddenly confronted by five Rolands, a very fast type of German scout, much faster indeed than his. He thought his situation anything but a happy one, but put on a bold face and headed in the most determined manner for the five Huns.

When he got close to them he bent down, and seizing the lower handle of the gun mounting, slid the gun up a matter of about two feet. This phenomenon, seen at close range as it was by the enemy, greatly disconcerted them, and each man probably thought that this remarkable gun mounting was some new deviltry on our part and determined not to be the first German to be shot down by it, with the remarkable result that our astonished pilot beheld them all turn around and beat it for all they were worth!

The Flying Corps behind the lines was also represented by a large number of our valiant friends in the Kite Balloon Corps, who were daily most gallantly seasick for six hours at a stretch as they hung from their sausages three or four thousand feet above the earth, endeavouring to detect gun flashes and the like and being shot at by all sorts of guns and experiencing all kinds of mainly beastly weather. The only consolation was that they were sincerely pitied by everyone.

On the German side of the lines the sight was very different, for the country appeared to be absolutely deserted and no convoys or troops apparently moved, a restriction of movement which was more than rendered necessary by the quantities of our aircraft which hourly patrolled every square mile of his country and exercised an observation from which little escaped, while on the other handy our side of the lines being quite free from Hun aircraft of any description, we were able to do whatever we pleased even within gun range, for the Hun artillery having no one to observe the targets or range in them if they were found, was powerless and could but fire promiscuously, a waste of ammunition scarcely justified considering that they were being forced back mile by mile the whole time.

Their whole country looked dead by day, but at night, of course, things were very different Every road or path was crowded to its utmost capacity by transports and troops, the shepherding of which must have taxed the most patient Teuton organisers, as, being unable to move by day without being blown sky-high, they had to crowd all their work into the hours of darkness. But even then they were not left in peace, far on every moonlight night it was the custom of some of our pilots to sally forth accompanied by an observer and with large quantities of ammunition, and fly very low up and down along these overcrowded roads and do their utmost to upset the Hun apple-cart as completely as possible.

Now consider—suppose you were a poor devil of the German cannon-fodderite, endeavouring to entice a large and overcrowded motor truck along a squelching morass of greasy mud, flanked on either side by a yawning ditch, with an indefinite amount of trucks, guns, and cursing infantry in front and an equally large amount behind, sliding and slithering and zigzagging your horrible way on a three-ton lorry. Alternately an excitable Prussian *ober-lieutenant* curses you on one side and a big *alte-leute* sergeant on the other, both threatening to blow your brains out for doing what the other told you to do. Every minute you drive you get closer to the thousands of brilliant shell bursts which you can see ahead of you so cunningly arranged for your destruction.

Then add to this happy scene an infernal aeroplane, which appears perhaps twenty feet above you and puts about three bullets in your stomach before you have finished your first curse, following this pleasantry up by a little playful business with the rest of the column to the complete and lasting discomfiture of the latter which, rapidly transforming itself into a sort of Irish stew of exceedingly muddy vehicles and men, is reluctantly compelled to await the dawn and then try and sort itself out. When the dawn comes it is generally of the hopeless variety, for another infernal aeroplane will appear, spot the mess, and turn some ten batteries on it in the twinkling of an eye, which transforms the Irish stew into a kind of weak porridge.

The net result is that the already hungry and emaciated Attilas in the front line take another cinch in their belts and fervently wish that they could get across to the company of the well fed carcasses of the British and be made prisoners!

In addition to these joyful excursions the Flying Corps carried out a great number of well planned bombing excursions by night, directed against numerous masses of material and Hun treasure trove, upon which a deep impression was generally left. Full many a Hun, sleeping peacefully in rest billets way back behind the lines before he took part in the next victory, was gratuitously presented with a large fat bomb, which had an unpleasant habit of going off violently when it hit his little paradise, when it was a case of Paradise Lost with a vengeance.

Railway trains also received impulses other than those designed for them, engines and trucks very often forsaking their steel rails and pretending to be aeroplanes under the direction of a two-hundredweight bomb; or again, large stores of shells, got together with much patient zeal and brain racking organisation, developed the habit of all going off together long before their owners intended them to, being enticed into such unpatriotic action by the example of one of our bombs! A fact which, although possessing a great amount of humour as far as we are concerned, can have been anything but comic to the vengeful disciples of Krupp who accompanied them.....

However, we know that matter is indestructible, and we are therefore hopeful that these gentlemen are not now in a position to suffer from cold feet.

Returning to daylight work, some (for the Hun succeedingly evil) genius thought of a job called contact patrol, the ramifications of which must have caused the gentle Hun more sheer rage than anything else the corps did, for the reason that the machines engaged in it had a habit of becoming so abusively personal in their work, the abuse taking a form of a stream of well directed and highly speedy machine gun bullets.

The most delightful side of contact patrol was the ground scouting behind the lines, when a machine went over very low and cruised about hopefully looking for something to destroy. Again taking a Hun point of view, one's nerve is considerably shaken when chased by one of these enthusiasts, for if one elects to try and escape one has to take into consideration one's large heavy trench boots and the juicy stretch of mud which forms the running track. One's fleeting footsteps therefore lightly skim the earth—through the mud—at a good three miles per hour, while the plane, being able to do one hundred and thirty with perfectly consummate ease, renders the chase unpleasantly exhausting, while on the other hand if one elects to stand still without adopting the formality of becoming forced to by your own exertions, you become a horribly easy target for each machine gun bullet, which scatters the mud up around you and thus enables the gunner to correct his aim to a nicety, to your eternal undoing.

It is when the Tommies actually leave that muddy trough of death called the first line trench, and walk forward through the counter-barrage, that the contact patrol machine comes into its own.

Flying low over the infernal tornado which yet again racks men and earth, the pilot and observer watch every move of the enemy, trying to counter his every effort, do anything and everything they can to give our boys a better chance. Not only do they form the eyes of the artillery, but take a hand (and a strong hand at that) themselves. It may be well to explain the part they are called upon to play when the big show is actually in progress. After hours, perhaps days, of intense artillery preparation, or barrage fire, the day dawns when the actual attack is to be made. The advance commences at what is called zero time (that is to say, if the first wave of the attack goes over at 6 a. m. it goes over officially at 0 a. m.). This system is rendered necessary by the need for minutely accurate synchronisation, by which means the cooperation between units of the attacking forces themselves, and between them and the artillery, is obtained with very nearly the certitude of a railway time table. Let us watch the attack in, let us say, one sector alone.

Just after dawn, and a little before zero time, will appear the aeroplane allotted to that particular part of the great battle. The infantry, crouching in their trenches under the hell of the counter-barrage, making their last preparations before going over, recognise its number, of which they have been previously informed, and proceed to establish communication, which may either be with electric lamps, or with what is called a panel, which consists of a contrivance like a Venetian blind, the slats showing black or white according to how they are turned; in both systems the Morse code will be used.

The whole time the aeroplane flies over the trenches it will not only be vigorously machine-gunned by the Boche, but run the double risk of stopping one of the flights of shells which scream over No Man's Land from friend and foe. As these shells are actually seen by the airman, not only singly, but in coveys, they remove any possibility there might exist of his being bored!

At length, after what has seemed an eternity to the overstrained participants, Briton and Hun, infantryman and airman, comes zero time. The troops commence to walk across the sea of mud, mangled humanity and wire, until at 2½ (two and one-half minutes from zero time, in reality two and a half minutes past six) they come to what is officially designated as the enemy front line. Just before they get to it, the artillery, working by time table, will lift the drum fire back towards the second line, and thus the famous creeping barrage will commence. The troops will continue walking (not running) behind the barrage as the latter is moved steadily on, keeping as close to it as they dare. It is now that the services of the contact patrollers become especially useful.

From the machine the pilot will see a number of objects of indefinite colour crawl out of their front line and struggle towards the enemy. From time to time one of the moving smudges will stop, and soon the sea of mud will be dotted with dead and wounded men. As the attacking wave gets closer to the Boche front line, the barrage will lift backward from it. With surprising suddenness little lanes will be created through our infantry and bunches will be seen to lose all appearance of action and sink to the ground, as if swept thither by some vast and unseen hand. But to a pilot of experience there is no mystery! It means that the Boches have brought a machine gun into action from the dugout where it and its gunners lay more or less safe under our barrage, and are sweeping a deadly stream over the attacking force.

There will ensue a few seconds' frantic search up and down the inferno of flame and smoke until the emplacement is spotted, then the nose of the machine swings down, there will be a scream of wind through the wires as the machine hurtles down at the hostile gun, a rapid confused stutter from the Vickers' guns, a terrific pressure of the feet against the floor as the machine swings up out of its dive, a momentary picture of a few huddled grey forms hanging over what looks like a thick walking stick, and the enemy's gun is out of action.

Sometimes the enemy's gun cannot be so easily dealt with—it may have an armoured head cover, for instance. The aeroplane's wireless will start tapping out its message to the artillery way back behind their lines. There will be a short pause, and then a rain of shells will tear up the earth all around the cause of the trouble. But machine guns are only one of the many jobs which fall to our pilot's lot. As the attack develops the artillery have great difficulty in ascertaining exactly where our front line is—telephone wires are shot away again and again, message bearers killed, colour lights not understood—a hundred things may happen—but the aeroplane, flying low over the scene, is able to locate our most advanced parties, who inform the pilot of their whereabouts by some prearranged system of signals, and will wireless back the information to the proper quarter. All things being equal, this will obviate our men being caught by our own shell fire.

Tempting targets, such as communication or other trenches, black with nice fat juicy Huns, receive instant and adequate attention from the aeroplane, either by means of bomb or machine gun; an offensive tactic which not only is of material value in the shape of Hun corpses, but greatly demoralises the rest of the enemy.

As their trenches are blown to pieces and spread all over the place in powder, the Boche will fortify shell craters and link them together. Then again he has to contend with very difficult circumstances, principally related to a machine capable of over one hundred miles an hour and possessing two expert machine gunners. The Hun, unable to rise from the ground for fear of being shot by our infantry, is reluctantly compelled to wallow in the mud until such time as the aerial gunners correct their aim by the little splotches of mud their bullets kick up, and succeed in putting him out of his misery.

Proceeding along from shell hole to shell hole, the gunner uses up a good many drums of ammunition, and demoralises the enemy in a way which could only be understood if one were in their wretched predicament Any concentration of troops will cause the sending back of an urgent signal to the artillery, who are eagerly on the *qui vive* for such a piece of luck...

Yes, contact patrol is quite interesting. The fact that one kills so many people with such comparative ease is very soothing, and does much to alleviate one's feelings about the hundreds of machine gun bullet holes which are dotted about all over the machine. To see an aeroplane come in after two hours of this work, and to examine it very closely, makes a man wonder whether the age of miracles is really past. Through the wings, through the body, sometimes a bare inch or so from the pilot, are scores of little holes, such as might be made by a child jabbing a lead pencil through the fabric as quickly as she could to the minute. More often than not the burst can be traced right across a wing. Vital control wires, fuel supplies, controlling surfaces, are chipped about and sometimes broken, or all but broken. There is no logical reason in the world why the machine does not fall to pieces over the trenches, and no calculation to justify the fact that the pilot was able to fly it back and get it down to the earth again.

But yet he does!

In one air battle alone thirty-seven Huns were engaged by twenty-four of ours and the battle was fought to a finish. In another case six of our machines met eight Hun scouts and fought until every machine on both sides had been either shot down, crippled, or forced out of action in some way. At fifteen thousand, at ten thousand, at five thousand and even lower, all along the Front, hundreds of such battles were in progress all day long, for we never left the sky unoccupied, one patrol going up and relieving another so that a constant sentry-go was maintained. One justly celebrated officer even flew far over into Hun territory and attacked the Germans on their own aerodrome, pouncing down on the machines as they left the earth to get up to him. It was rumoured at the time that he went to the enemy training aerodromes and shot down the pupils as they tried to do their first flights! Olympus, however, did not have anything to say officially about the matter.

A friend of mine who happened to be flying over the scene of earlier Somme violence one April, perpetrated a joke on the Germans which they possibly never appreciated. He and his observer obtained a large football and painted "April Fool" on it in German. On the afternoon of April lst they sailed over the lines to a large town some way back, and flying low, dropped the football into the Grand Place. The Huns, seeing this large and fearsome bomb dropping majestically down upon them, thought it a species of frightfulness excelling anything we had ever done, and rushed to the shelter of the houses surrounding the square. When the much dreaded bomb *did* hit it bounced nearly one hundred feet into the air, and kept on bouncing until it finally came to rest, when it was cautiously approached by the unromantic and humour-lacking Teutons!

My friend did not stay much longer, as the Huns, with great lack of sportsmanship, kept a vigorous machine gun fire at him, so he returned to tell the tale in whispers. Any description of the Somme scrapping would be incomplete without a word of reference to the way the Flying Corps dealt with the enemy kite balloons. These singular and humorous aerial vehicles gave the impression of a large German sausage which had been well pumped up and weighted at one end. They hung some two or three thousand feet over their winches, ready to be hauled in at the slightest sign of frightfulness on our part. As they formed a distinct menace to our operations it was determined to make a concerted attack upon them all along the line. This was done, and to my knowledge eleven were shot down within two hours, the assailants using their very best wiles to catch the enemy unawares.

I have said before that to approach an enemy balloon was merely to cause its rapid "reeling in" to the ground, where it sat and waited until we went away. One of our bright sparks went over very high up and pretended to be hit by the enemy Archie, who was shooting at him. Tumbling over and over, spinning this way and that, he brought the machine the whole way down in the most lifelike imitation of a "direct hit." The Hun balloon, not unnaturally, suspected nothing. Just before he got to the balloon, however, the pilot righted the machine, dived at the balloon and got in a double drum of tracer ammunition, with the result that the balloon came down in flames. Others flew over very low down and arrived between the balloon and its winch. The wretched Teuton balloonist was then faced with the pleasing alternative of being reeled down, in which case the aeroplane, not having so far to climb, shot him down all the quicker, or else he chose to remain where he was, in which case he had all the further to drop!

Balloon strafing is a little sport with a science all to itself, and many and many a tale could be told about the ways and means that the corps had adopted.

But perhaps this at another time.

Out of the terrific surging maelstrom of fighting, and the clashing din of great exploits, it is only possible to memorise a lamentably small amount of instances. But yet, as at no other time in its previous history, did the Flying Corps prove what wonderful cooperation could accomplish and what the highest degree of personal daring was capable of bringing about. Our casualties were heavy, but the casualties of the enemy much, much heavier. The enemy was unable to protect his troops or grant ground observation to his artillery. The Flying Corps was able to go over the lines where it pleased, meet the opposition, and overcome it. The opinion of the German soldiers in the forefront of battle was very recognisable in the scores of letters, notes, diaries, etc., which were taken from the dead and living by our Intelligence department and published. One and all bitterly complained of the constant and pitiless persecution of our machines and deplored—nay, sometimes cursed—their own flying service.

For all their vaunted aerial supremacy, the enemy was absolutely unable to hold us, and our squadrons always, and at all times, did their jobs, flying at all times over enemy territory. Engine failure, a wound, an unlucky shot, meant being taken prisoner or worse, if such is possible; their casualties were heavy, as I have said, but methinks the corps indeed had the greater share of glory.

CHAPTER 14

The Red Cross Machine

The Casualty Clearing Station had been improvised in an old French prison just outside the town, and was surrounded by a broad moat A little offshoot from the main road led over a small iron bridge and through a great forbidding stone gateway, which was flanked by a large guard house also of stone, but the rusty iron gates were permanently padlocked back to the walls, a large Red Cross swung over them, and the sentry at the gate was no longer the grim warder with his bunch of keys, but instead a cheery British Tommy.

Inside the old walls were paths and courtyards of white cobble stones somewhat overgrown with moss about the edges, and shaded by one or two huge trees, under which in warm weather there was usually a little fleet of wheeled chairs, occupied by jocular but pale and thin men clothed in pyjamas, numerous rugs, and the inevitable "fag," who, if it were morning, were invariably engaged with the great event of the day—the arrival of the English papers

The event had three phases: It commenced with numbers of trenchant prophecies upon the day's developments of whatever situation the speaker was following, it might be a murder trial, the form of a race horse, the Premier's last speech; then, as the excitement of anticipation reached fever heat, the daily millennium would come to pass, in the shape of the advent of a small and very business like *garçon*, on a bicycle so dilapidated that it was a source of fresh wonder every morning it appeared. The boy was then swallowed up by a crowd of eager Tommies, some hobbling, some quite lively, and some barely able to move, but everyone who could escape his eagle-eyed nurse and crawl to the paper boy before the precious papers were sold out did so. There followed about an hour's unbroken silence while the news was devoured for it was the code that silence was a *sine qua non*; then discussion once more burst into full flame, while the destinies of the entire empire were once and for all outlined and settled.

Set around the courtyards and paths were numerous brick barracks of incredibly cold and cheerless design, but with their gloom somewhat mitigated by the efforts of the nurses and orderlies. Each long barrack room was occupied by a closely placed line of beds on either side, and one or two long narrow tables in the centre, on which there were generally tin cans full of flowers, and a few books and magazines. At the side of each bed was a tiny square table, the under part of which formed a cupboard for the patient's knickknacks, while over the head of the bed hung details of the patient's condition. The bare whitewashed walls and wooden floors of the old place were, if nothing else, spotlessly clean. A small building in the centre of the place had been fitted up as a surgery, and part of one of the larger buildings was used for the staff quarters.

The officers' ward was situated in a sort of grim cavern with stone arches and curved white-washed ceiling, in the recesses of which the evening candle light threw weird shadows. Upstairs, over this ward, was a smaller room furnished with wicker and canvas deck chairs, a table and a number of books, for use as a kind of day room by those officers well enough to be up. But owing to a steady increase of patients this had to be made into a ward also. Each officer had a little table like the men, and the "Wanted in Cabin" part of his kit was placed underneath his bed. There were quite a number of books to read, the food was good, and plenty of it for the lucky people who were on full diet. The day nurse came on duty at 8 o'clock in the morning and the night nurse at 8 o'clock in the evening. We had breakfast at about 7:45 a.m., lunch at 1, a cup of tea (Aha!) at 4 o'clock, and supper at 7.

The patients themselves hailed from all branches of the army and a good many sections of the Front, and even the Canal Transport Section was represented by an officer who had fallen off his barge into a canal and contracted pneumonia! Then there were two machine gun officers fresh from the Loos salient, complete with Boche bullet each, a Royal Army Medical Corps officer just up from six weeks between-the-lines work on the Somme, who was half mad with shell shock, a cheerful and canny captain of the Gordon Highlanders, an officer of the Devon regiment with artistic tendencies in the direction of pen and ink sketching, and two specimens from the Flying Corps.

The commanding officer was an elderly and kindly major, who, although his intentions were of the best, one day made a bad *faux pas*.

Entering the ward he was led by the nurse to a bed whereon was a recumbent figure bandaged almost from head to foot, but still quite conscious.

"This is a Flying Corps officer, just come in," she told the medical officer.

The medical officer, gazing at the injured man, remarked mildly, "Oh, a flying officer? Tell me, *did you fall?*"

A lack of logical reasoning which was rather tactless!

The Gordon Highlander had brought a faithful body servant with him, and the latter was often despatched into town to purchase dainties for the delectation of the ward, a particular *pièce-de-resistance* being an enormous fondant containing an entire walnut, the taste of which lingers yet. The lad fra' Aberdeen was unable to speak a word of French, but always succeeded in purchasing what was needed. Once an evening was brightened by an excellent concert given in a large marquee specially erected in the courtyard for the purpose.

Sometimes the Gordons, Devons and the Flying Corps would hold a debate, one of the number stating a thesis which the other two attacked, to the huge enjoyment of everyone. A good deal of reading and sleeping went on; and in general all jogged along like a number of Micawbers, "waiting for something to turn up."

One morning something did, in the form of a hurriedly organised evacuation to the base of a number of officers, who wallowing peacefully in bed at 8:30 a. m., were by 9:30 sitting or lying in motor ambulances ready to start for the hospital train. At about 9:45 the ambulance pushed off and we sped rapidly along the interminably straight stretch of pave to a railway depot, at which we arrived in about half an hour's time, and found waiting for us a long, grey painted English train with the Red Cross emblazoned on the sides of each coach, where we immediately became the object of the solicitude of one of the most considerate and courteous medical officers it has ever been my fortune to meet.

We had by now realised that we had been caught up by a most thoughtful, vast, and accurate machine, which had gripped hold of us at the casualty clearing station, and intended to conduct the whole of our affairs until it saw us once more fit and well and back on duty. Everything in the train was obviously the outcome of a great deal of experience of handling wounded and a very keen desire to make them as happy as was possible.

The medical officer now proceeded to take down our names and particulars of our cases, especially diet, the last named being obviously a necessary procedure for we should probably be on the train a good long time. We were then classified into three main classes: "Walking," "Sitting," and "Lying," which meant that the last two types were carried everywhere while the walking cases proceeded under their own steam.

These simple formalities over, we were ushered into a coach, and our kit into a baggage van. The interior of the coach was lined with bunks, two rows a side, one on top of the other, the top bunk folding back so that the bottom one could be used as a seat if necessary. The bunks on all one side of the coach had been raised in this manner and a narrow table bolted down in front of them. In racks at either end of the coach were quantities of books, magazines, newspapers, playing cards, chess, draughts, dominoes, and a large assortment of puzzles, the latter being much favoured by hospital authorities for the purpose of amusing and soothing patients, but which in many cases reduce the latter to tears of mortification when they are completely baffled after hours of patient endeavours to solve them.

Fresh ambulances now began to arrive every few minutes, the drivers reporting to the medical officer or his non-commissioned officer, who took up his station a little way from the train and then directed the ambulance to the proper coach, to which it would draw up, backwards, opposite the main door in the centre, and the cases were lifted out, examined, and carefully placed in bunks, where they were immediately attended to by the many nurses on the train; while other ambulances brought sitting and walking cases, amongst whom there presently appeared a pilot from an artillery squadron which we always escorted, who was suffering from an absolute wreckage of nerves after nine months' continuous flying.

In about two hours' time the stream of ambulances ceased and shortly after this the long train steamed quietly out of the little country station and began its journey back to the base. The last sight I had of the Front was a formation from our squadron flying up towards the Archie-spotted sky over the lines, the strong sunlight catching their polished planes and reflecting in brilliant gleams, until somehow, in spite of their strictly utilitarian garb of grey and chocolate paint, they looked beautiful.

Soon after our departure a number of Royal Army Medical Corps orderlies appeared and began to set out the necessary implements for lunch, which pleasant occurrence was followed by a still pleasanter one, for a smiling ward sister appeared with a note book and asked each of us what we would like to drink!

"Now what would you like?"

"Oh, everything you've got, sister—bottled Bass, Pomeroy, claret, old port, whiskey—just mix them all up together, sister, and leave me to it!"

The sister laughed merrily.

"Horrible man! I'll give you a bottle of Bass—but, oh, just a minute. You don't look very well—in fact, you look jolly bilious! What's your diet!"

"On full diet, sister."

"Let me see your case card!"

He unwillingly produced it and she gave it a brief glance.

"Oh, you naughty boy! Why didn't you tell the truth just once to see what it felt like?"

"Just plain water for this officer, orderly!"

After a jolly good lunch everyone settled down to boa-constrict behind the inevitable cigarettes—even these, by the way, had been provided by the thoughtful medical officer in charge of the train—and the Flying Corps pilots were soon deep in a conversation mainly consisting of retrospective shop. Throughout the afternoon the train stopped at little rural railway stations, in which a line of ambulances were invariably waiting. The speed and consummate gentleness with which the wounded were swiftly transferred from the ambulances, taken off the stretcher, put in bed, attended to by a nurse and probably given something to eat and drink, was a fresh wonder to us at every station. At every fresh halt we saw the great Red Cross machine gather up to itself more and more patients with the same accuracy with which it had engulfed us.

Despite the fact that they had been handling thousands and thousands of cases throughout the war, all the Royal Army Medical Corps, from the youngest orderly to the officer commanding the train, were wonderfully human and quick to realise the wounded Tommie's point of view, and tried to make his short stay with them as complete a metamorphosis as possible from the hell that he had just left. None of their requests seemed too much trouble to attend to, but yet they allowed nothing to interfere with the most important business on hand.

At about dusk the medical officer came along after a particularly long halt and told us that the train had now its full burden and that we were off straight for the base. Soon after this we were served with dinner, about 7 o'clock, and dozed on and off throughout the evening while the train rumbled monotonously on in the direction of Staples. At about midnight the train came to a halt in the midst of apparently a great town, for thousands upon thousands of shimmering lights dotted the darkness around. After a very brief wait we were taken from the coach and placed in the ambulances.

The scene outside was one which made the most powerful impression upon me that I had ever received—an impression which I shall never forget and can never adequately describe.

Under the glare of the hissing and spluttering electrics, hung from great posts, lay the long grey train, its Red Crosses showing faintly in the artificial light, every window alight and admitting sight of the white garbed nurses and orderlies hurrying about inside. A great open stretch of beaten gravel ran alongside the train, chilled with the sweep of the night December wind from the north, occupied by streams of ambulances coming and going with their freights of battered and worn humanity; their drivers coming to pass a word or two with the train sister—drivers of all descriptions.

The ordinary cockney driver with his raucous, cheery greeting; then the wealthy owner of his own ambulance—the driving of which was the only occupation health or age allowed him to follow for the war; large numbers of slim khaki-clad girls, ladies who had often brought their own ambulances with them from America, Canada, or Britain; the passage of numbers of stretchers with their white, blanket-clad, immobile figures from train to car; the thousands of shimmering lights, now revealed as an endless array of hutments; and over all the bustling, striving spirit of war, sleepless, aware....

It was a scene to engrave itself upon the memory forever for it was so unreal, and yet so real.

We had a short run in the ambulance over a dead smooth road—even the road the machine had thought of—and arrived outside a long wooden shed. This shed was already peopled by quite a number of cases, some walking, and some lying on the ground on stretchers. Each patient in his turn either walked or was carried in front of a large table at which sat a Royal Army Medical Corps doctor and two sergeants, where the particulars of the patient were ascertained and the number of his ward stated to his bearers or guide. The captain and the two sergeants were working at very high pressure, but always with the same sure method which characterised everything the machine did.

Our little party was soon passed through, although no more preference was shown to an officer than to a man, unless the former was in a much more serious condition, and we went along the hut into a long wooden corridor, out of which doors opened into more large huts at right angles to it.

Two of us were handed over to the nurse in charge of Ward C, who proceeded to deal with us with the utmost kindness and efficiency—with a coolness, in fact, which led to us asking her how she managed it. Yes, the machine had thought of everything! She had known beforehand exactly how many patients were coming into the ward, what time they would arrive and approximately what condition to expect them in, and had made her arrangements accordingly. I was led to a bed with the sheets turned back ready for entrance, a foot-warmer in position, a pair of clean pyjamas—carefully warmed—laid out on the pillow, a table beside the bed with a shaded electric light, a large glass of hot milk, and a magazine, should the patient feel too excited to sleep, in which case he could read and thus be calmed down.

A pair of warm slippers were underneath the bed and a dressing gown hanging beside it. A few yards away was the open door of a bathroom—even the bath full of hot water! Nothing was forgotten, nothing had to be waited for. The nurse was ready, cool, capable. Even in the few moments while I gazed with startled amazement at this preparedness she had made herself master of the case chart, knew my diet, and inquired whether "I'd like a bath and would I prefer a hot whiskey and lemon to the milk?"

Once more startled, I gave the usual Flying Corps answer to such a question! After I had had a topping bath, the hot toddy, and some biscuits, had snuggled down between the warm clean sheets and read for half an hour, she came round to ask me how I felt, and if there was anything I could think of I wanted.

"Now you're quite sure, laddie, that there is nothing else you want? All right, I'll put the lamp out, then."

In the bed next to me lay a very young officer, apparently seriously wounded, for every now and again he could not repress a low groan, half sigh, as he moved his thin white arms restlessly about the coverlet. The nurse went over and bent down over him—oh, she was a dear! Her kindly face showed a deal, for all its sympathy, of the things she had seen in the past two years; she was about thirty-five or forty, probably with children of her own—

"Well, kiddy, do you feel restless just now?"

"Yes, nurse. I can't sleep, my head will buzz and I am so hot—hot—"

His voice trailed off and he weakly plucked the sheets back from his chest. The nurse bent down and quietly kissed his forehead.

"Poor boy," she whispered softly as she leaned over him. . . . The shaded ward light just irradiated his handsome boyish face—he was only a child—his white neck and clean young body—

Oh God, why was war?

The next day more patients came in and some went out—screens would be put around a bed, the medical officer would come in, disappear behind them more frequently than usual, and the next morning the screens had gone and the bed, with clean sheets and clothes, was awaiting a fresh patient . . . After four days at Etaples a whole party of us were evacuated for England. Each officer had two little envelopes of transparent paper tied on to his coat buttons or shoulder straps, inside which were the details of the case so folded that the patient's ailments could be instantly read through the envelope and its statement examined! All cases to be entrained were taken through a wooden hut, open at both ends, in the middle of which stood a medical officer who examined and reported the particulars from each envelope.

Lieut. A——, G. S. wound, right shoulder, serious.

Capt B——, shock and P. U. O.

Second Lieut. C——, G. S. wounds, head and left arm.

And so on and so on; G. S. meaning gun shot, while other letters stood for trench fever and the like. After this examination all the patients were placed on a hospital train which shortly after moved off on its journey to the port of embarkation. The arrangements in the train were just as thorough as in the first one we had boarded and everyone was as kind and courteous as ever; there was a deal of speculation as to whether we were bound for Calais or Boulogne, but even then the general sentiment was evidenced by a weak voice issuing from yards of bandages occupying one of the bunks:

"I don't care a damn whether we are going from Calais or Marseilles, by balloon or submarine, as long as we get safely to dear old Blighty!"

As the train went along, now in broad daylight, we were all amazed by the gigantic size of the huge base depots we passed through, and by the extraordinarily heavy traffic on the railway—interminably long trains of guns on trucks, horses, shells, men, packing cases, crates—

everything on a scale much too vast for us to grasp. Also by the great hospitals which lined the seashore all along our route—-all, we knew by hearsay, full up; and as at no other time we began to have a dim idea of the immensity of the undertaking in which we were involved. No one who has not seen these bases, these continuous streams of trains, with thousands upon thousands of horses, men and guns, countless tons of stores and shells, the great camps of wood and stone, the permanent, determined look of everything, can realise how immense the operations of the British Expeditionary Forces really are.

About 5 o'clock the train meandered into a city and finally drew up on a quay, alongside a large white ship with great crosses painted on her sides, and soon, under the aegis of numerous medical officers, our train began to disgorge its human cargo, who were laid on other stretchers on the quay beside the gangway and then carried aboard, particulars being taken as each case went over the gangway. Numerous motor ambulances began to arrive with quantities of wounded, and they, too, were swallowed up by the white ship; great numbers of the ambulance drivers were ladies who had to stand about and smilingly undergo the concentrated stares of scores of eyes, as the owners hungrily drank in the sight of an English girl! A grizzled old sergeant, the stump of one arm swathed in bandages, called out from his stretcher to a tall, fresh young driver of a Ford ambulance:

"Ah, lassie, do ye come and let me see ye close to, lassie! Come now, it's juist ower th' ro'd, hinny!"

She blushingly complied, and the grizzled old veteran, who hadn't seen his native Northumberland or any other part of England for a year or more, gazed at her in undisguised admiration! All these fair Jehus and Ford Boadiceas seemed most extraordinarily pretty, and the walking cases became almost unruly when the medical officer wouldn't let them off the ship to go and talk to them. . .

The ship had been fitted out most thoroughly for the Red Cross, and was one network of bunks. At either end of the ship was a large hatchway with a smooth-running electric elevator, in which the stretchers were placed and lowered to which ever deck was their destination. A large supply of books and the inevitable puzzles were on hand, arrangements for food most complete, the nurses as ubiquitous as ever, and down to the minutest detail the machine once more displayed its grasp of facts.

Lights out was at 9 p.m. and at 4 a.m. all the walking cases were rooted out of their bunks to make way for a fresh influx of more seriously hurt patients. These were got aboard with great rapidity, the ship cleared the harbour and steamed away for England about 6 a.m. In half an hour we came in sight of the white cliffs of Dover gleaming in the rising sun, while astern the low lying land of France merged into a purple and blue haze.

All the patients were now fearfully excited, and all those well enough to be on deck gazed eagerly at England as if they expected that it might be swallowed up any instant before their longing eyes. Overstrained nerves began to get very worried on the subject of mines and U-boats, for as regards the latter, no one felt exactly positive of the safety our Red Crosses should have given us, for the Hun is a ruthless gentleman and in his grasp of great affairs proves to ignore little trifles like Red Crosses! *Gott strafe England!*

Two of our destroyers passed close by us, and those of their crew on deck sent a ringing cheer across the water as they shot by; farther over we passed a large white ship like our own, with enormous Red Crosses painted on her sides, going back empty for a fresh cargo from France; at about 7:30 we moved in Dover Harbour alongside three long hospital trains with engines attached, which the machine had installed there in readiness for us; then the electric elevators got busy, and stretcher after stretcher disappeared into the trains until they had all been moved, when the walking cases were attended to. As we entered the train our faithful little envelopes were once more scanned and a record taken.

At 9 o'clock the train drew out and steamed rapidly away along the main line to London, the track being kept open for it—always the case with a hospital train, to which ordinary traffic give preference at all times. A light lunch of coffee and sandwiches backed up by a box of cigarettes was brought round by the orderlies, and nurses flitted round tending to the more serious cases.

At 11 o'clock the long train glided over the Thames by the Charing Cross Bridge and slid gently in under the great glass domed roof of Charing Cross station. The second the train came to a standstill an alert official of the St. John's Ambulance Society stepped into the coach and produced a large book of canvas pages possessing slits, each slit containing a paper slip onto which by some occult means had been described the case and name of each officer in the coach. We had all thought ourselves rather *blasé* about the remarkable stunts the machine pulled off; but this last one completely took the wind out of our sails, and as someone remarked: "It was blooming weird!"

The St. John's official then worked like lightning with the walking cases. He asked each officer his name, consulted his book, produced a slip which he gave to the officer, and then handed him over to a waiting myrmidon, who led him away out of the coach. Outside were parked vast quantities of ambulances, and near the rear of the train a long line of limousines.

Four minutes after the train stopped another officer and I were seated inside a huge Rolls Royce limousine—lent, of course, to the Red Cross for this kind of work. The chauffeur was handed another slip indicating our destination, and we slid smoothly and expensively from the station. In the courtyard outside was a great cheering, singing mob, who crowded round each car as it came out and thrust great bundles of flowers—the costly blooms of the affluent and the humble meadow flowers of the poor—and huge boxes of chocolates into the car, laughing and crying and cheering madly....

Our destination proved to be a small private hospital in the West End, where we were once more expected and all our wants anticipated. Our hostess, like hundreds—no, thousands—of ladies all over Britain, was living in a small section of her great house, while the rest of it had been fitted up as a hospital. So we were at last Home! The machine had pursued its well oiled running and had delivered us safely into the heart of England, and even there it still exerted a constant watchfulness over our welfare until it finally saw its *protégés* once more back in harness.

The wonder of the Red Cross has not yet faded one particle in my memory. Calm and unhurrying, it never got itself into a mess by trying to achieve the impossible, yet to its magnificent organisation, no obstacle had a moment's chance. The speed with which it worked was well evidenced in its handling of the casualties of the Vimy Ridge show, when men who were wounded just after dawn were in London hospitals late the same afternoon. It never failed and it was never too machine-like to be at all times human. When we looked back and reflected upon what must be the enormous cost of the upkeep of its vast and expensive organisation, we were possessed of a wild desire to donate every bean we had, and then rush out and hold up London at the point of a Lewis and make it disgorge every penny it had to an institution the activities of which it did not even barely comprehend.

Of the women—of the gallant girls who work their fingers to the bone and their nerves to destruction for the welfare of the British Tommy and his officers—well, ask any wearer of a wound stripe. Suffice to say that to he under their care and to see their work forever shames, in a man's eyes, the strong, healthy woman, unfettered by circumstances, who "doesn't think she could bear the sights," etc.—who *could*, but *won't*.

As regards the men of the R.A.M.C. the list of decorations tells its own tale, but here again ask a returned man, who, although to whom the sight of the most extreme bravery is the veriest commonplace, will invariably pay their stretcher bearers and doctors the highest compliment that can be paid to man....

And so this miserably inadequate tale of an infinitesimal part of the work of the Great Corps is finished. I am sitting in the mess on another and newer squadron, on the edge of a group around the fire. Men we knew in the old days have changed now—instead of single "pips" on their shoulders, I now see three of them and sometimes a crown, as they all talk together through the hazy smoke about the things that are, and the things that were. As the evening lengthens on and the mess waiter begins switching off all the unneeded lights, a silence begins to fall on them, and the red leaping glare of the firelight illuminates their keen fearless faces and eyes that live again, in its red embers, those pulsing, thrilling moments of Life and Death two miles above Flanders.

www.ingramcontent.com/pod-product-compliance
Lightning Source LLC
Chambersburg PA
CBHW021003090426
42738CB00007B/626